The Next Ones

The
NEXT
ONES

How McDavid, Matthews
and a Group of Young Guns
Took Over the NHL

MICHAEL TRAIKOS

 Douglas &McIntyre

DOUGLAS AND MCINTYRE (2013) LTD.
P.O. Box 219, Madeira Park, BC, V0N 2H0
www.douglas-mcintyre.com

EDITED by Silas White
INDEXED by Allie Turner
TEXT DESIGN by Shed Simas / Onça Design
COVER DESIGN by Setareh Ashrafologhalai
PRINTED AND BOUND in Canada

Canada Council   Conseil des arts
for the Arts   du Canada

BRITISH COLUMBIA
ARTS COUNCIL
An agency of the Province of British Columbia

Douglas and McIntyre (2013) Ltd. acknowledges the support of the Canada Council for the Arts, which last year invested $153 million to bring the arts to Canadians throughout the country. We also gratefully acknowledge financial support from the Government of Canada and from the Province of British Columbia through the BC Arts Council and the Book Publishing Tax Credit.

LIBRARY AND ARCHIVES CANADA CATALOGUING IN PUBLICATION
Traikos, Michael, author
     The next ones : how McDavid, Matthews and a group of young guns took over the NHL / Michael Traikos.

Includes index.
Issued in print and electronic formats.
ISBN 978-1-77162-198-4 (softcover).--ISBN 978-1-77162-199-1 (HTML)

1. Hockey players--Biography. 2. National Hockey League. I. Title.

GV848.5.A1T73 2018   796.962092'2   C2018-903087-9
                                               C2018-903088-7

CONTENTS

For Danielle, my density—I mean, destiny

In memory of Fanny (Baba) Misketis, who passed
away while this book was being written and who
was so heavily involved in my own origin story.

FOREWORD

THE FIRST TIME I SAW CONNOR McDAVID PLAY LIVE was in the 2015 World Junior Championships in Toronto, where Canada won gold.

I'll never forget it.

It was the championship final and Canada was leading 2–1 against Russia in the second period when McDavid scored a goal that caused my jaw to drop. Taking a pass in the middle of the ice, he rocketed past two defenders for a breakaway and then snuck a shot through the Russian goalie's five-hole.

Everything about the goal was amazing.

Some players have two or three gears. McDavid seemed to have five or six with a nitro boost to spare. It was spectacular. I had seen his highlights on TV and YouTube. But watching him live was completely different. You got a real sense of his speed and skill and everything else that makes him so special.

All the players in this book share that same ability.

This is an amazing time for hockey. I don't think the game has ever been this good. The skill on display is really something else. The players are not only faster and stronger, but they're doing things that I didn't think were possible when I was playing.

You see smaller players like Mitch Marner or Johnny Gaudreau deke circles around defencemen and you can't help but marvel at what they are able to accomplish at their size. Back in the day, those guys simply weren't getting opportunities. Now, they're some of the NHL's brightest stars—and rightfully so.

What's really stood out from watching these players emerge—and reading about their origin stories—is how different each of them is. They play the game differently. And they've all followed a different path. In Auston Matthews's case, he had to carve out a path on his own. And that's what makes this next generation of next ones so impressive.

Like Mario Lemieux and Gordie Howe before me, I may have had an impact on the next generation of superstars through my on- and off-ice actions. But this isn't a cookie-cutter league. What works for one player doesn't always work for another.

Sure, it takes talent and a ton of hard work to even get to the NHL. But to become a star takes something else. Each of these players is so special, not just in his ability but in his drive. Whether it's McDavid taking hundreds of shots every day or Jack Eichel failing and then persevering against much older competition, nothing came easy to any of these players.

No one was an overnight success. No one got handed anything without putting in a ton of effort.

For most of them, they've always been in the spotlight. They've always had a target on their backs. But each one of them persevered to become one of the best in his generation. And they did it their own way. That's what's so interesting about this book.

Both McDavid and Aaron Ekblad entered the Ontario Hockey League (OHL) a year earlier than normal. I went in at age sixteen. Matthews grew up in Arizona and decided to play in Switzerland rather than in college. Matthews is a strong kid. He knew he could handle himself against men. You look at his neck and he's just going to get bigger and stronger.

That isn't the case with Marner and Gaudreau. You look at them and you wonder, how is it that they got here? And when you find out, you appreciate their journey even more.

All my life, everyone has given me the benefit of the doubt because of my physical appearance. I was always one of the biggest. With Marner and Gaudreau, it's the opposite. They've been doubted and disregarded almost every step of the way. In some ways, it's probably helped them get this far.

Even William Nylander had it hard. Don't think he was drafted just because his dad played in the NHL. In some ways, it was probably more difficult playing in his father's shadow. I can tell you this much: as good as Michael Nylander was, his son might be even more talented. And that's saying something.

And then there's Mark Scheifele. You look at him today and he's such a dominating centre. You figure he's always been this way. But then you realize it took him a long time to even get to the NHL. To me, that's even more impressive. He's like John LeClair. He was one of the best wingers I ever played with, but it took him a while to figure out just how good he was. When he eventually did, he and Mikael Renberg and I did great things together.

It's another way of saying that not every player's journey is a straight line. There are bumps and detours along the way. That goes for first-line stars as much as it does for the fourth-line grinders.

From McDavid to Matthews, I think it's great for hockey that there are so many young players already taking over the league. I wish them all the best. I really do.

And I can't wait to see the next generation of next ones who will follow in their path.

—ERIC LINDROS

Eric Lindros, who was a No. 1 overall pick in the 1991 draft, scored 372 goals and 865 points in 760 games over a Hall of Fame career that spanned thirteen years. A former Philadelphia Flyers captain, he won the Hart Memorial Trophy in 1994–95 and had his famed No. 88 jersey retired by the franchise in 2017.

INTRODUCTION

IT WAS SUPPOSED TO BE A GIMMICK. IT ENDED UP BECOMing a game-changer.

When the NHL and the NHL Players' Association decided to stage another World Cup of Hockey in the fall of 2016, the usual six powerhouses (Canada, the United States, Russia, Sweden, Finland and the Czech Republic) participated. But in the name of inclusion, the leftover European nations were lumped together on Team Euro, while Team North America collected the best Canadian- and American-born players who were age twenty-three or younger.

Whereas Team Euro surprised everyone and made the final against Canada, the young Team North America stars didn't even advance past the round robin. But with its black-and-bright-orange colour scheme and live-fast-die-young playing style, Team North America was the highlight of the tournament.

The kids were lightning quick, supremely skilled and full of spunk. They were also very, very fun. When the 5-foot-9, 157-pound Johnny Gaudreau was asked if he was worried about other teams trying to intimidate the younger players with bodychecks and physical play, he replied, "It's tough to hit someone you can't catch."

The idea for this book came from covering Team North America from the start of training camp to their final thrilling game of that two-week tournament. But really, the World Cup of Hockey was just the beginning.

A few weeks after Connor McDavid and Auston Matthews were teammates for the first—and last—time at an international event, the one hundredth year of the NHL began. It truly was a year for the ages. In celebrating the past, the league also looked forward to the future in a season where the kids took over.

McDavid, who was twenty years old and playing in his first full season, led all scorers with 100 points and won both the Hart Memorial Trophy and the Ted Lindsay Award as MVP. A teenaged Matthews won the Calder Trophy as the league's top rookie, while also tying for second among all players with 40 goals. Matt Murray, who was twenty-two when he won a Stanley Cup the previous spring, backstopped the Pittsburgh Penguins to a second consecutive championship while still technically a rookie. By the end of the season, seven of the top thirty scorers—including four of the top ten—were twenty-three years old or younger.

This isn't a top-ten list of the NHL's young players. There are names here that you will agree with and some that you will question. You might, for instance, be wondering why Vancouver's Brock Boeser or Edmonton's Leon Draisaitl *were* not included, or why so-and-so is here and Boston's David Pastrnak or Colorado's Nathan MacKinnon *are* not. I could go on and on.

From Florida's Aleksander Barkov and Columbus's Zach Werenski to Arizona's Clayton Keller and the Islanders' Michael Barzal, there are more than enough supremely talented young players to warrant another ten chapters. That's how stacked the league is with young talent.

All I'll say is that the names I chose made sense to me when the book was conceived and I think they still make sense now. At the same time, this isn't a book about what the players have done in the NHL. This is what they did to get there. Consider this book an origin story, where instead of Peter Parker getting bitten by a radioactive spider, it's how Matthews was bitten by the hockey bug while growing up in Scottsdale, Arizona.

Each story is different. Whereas Aaron Ekblad was always the biggest and strongest kid even while playing two years above his age group, a late bloomer like Mark Scheifele was continuously knocked around as he fought through obstacle after obstacle on his longer and more arduous path to the NHL.

You'll notice the narratives are far different than if this book had been written ten or twenty years ago. This generation isn't like the generation before it. The players didn't necessarily grow up skating on frozen ponds like Bobby Orr did. McDavid learned how to become the fastest and most agile hockey player in the world by strapping on rollerblades and deking around paint cans in his parents' two-car garage. Patrik Laine shot pucks at pop cans, William Nylander shot pucks at his dad's NHL buddies and Johnny Gaudreau chased Skittles around the ice.

Obvious thanks go to the players, their families and friends, and former coaches and teammates for helping reveal the secrets behind what has made each person so special. This book could not have been written without their co-operation, something I valued whether I was travelling to Thunder Bay to spend a low-key day with the Stanley Cup and Murray, or watching old YouTube clips of a pint-sized Mitch Marner with his parents.

Last but not least, thank you to whoever has purchased and decided to read my first book. I hope you enjoy these stories as much as I enjoy telling them.

— MICHAEL TRAIKOS, January 2018

Mark SCHEIFELE

WINNIPEG JETS

» № 55 «

POSITION	CENTRE
SHOOTS	RIGHT
HEIGHT	6′3″
WEIGHT	207 LB
BORN	MARCH 15, 1993
BIRTHPLACE	KITCHENER, ON, CAN
DRAFT	2011 WPG, 1ST RD, 7TH PK (7TH OVERALL)

Mark Scheifele and St. Louis Blues' Patrik Berglund prepare for a faceoff in 2018. AP Photo/Billy Hurst

OFTENTIMES IN HOCKEY, GREATNESS IS APPARENT the moment you see it. There's an "It" factor, something you can't always explain or fully understand, but that is undeniable to both the seasoned scout and casual fan watching for the first time. The scouts who first laid eyes on Crosby and McDavid and other phenoms knew they were seeing something special, even when the players were at their very youngest. These were hockey prodigies who were not only playing one or two years above their age level, but were dominating the competition. They made the game look easy.

When scouts first laid their eyes on Mark Scheifele, they didn't see someone who made the sport look easy. If anything, he made it look hard. "A tall, lanky kid who falls over a lot and is weak" was the scouting report Scheifele heard over and over again when he was trying to get drafted into the Ontario Hockey League (OHL). "I heard he got hurt a lot," said Barrie Colts general manager Jason Ford. "Someone said every game they went to he was lying on the ice."

That's not the image of Scheifele today. The late bloomer who was cut from his first junior training camp and sent back to the OHL twice is now "one of the best centres in the league," according to Toronto Maple Leafs and Team Canada head coach Mike Babcock. How did Scheifele do it? How did a player go from potential bust to "one of the best centres in the league"? He did it by becoming, in his own words, "a hockey nerd."

5

Mark SCHEIFELE

It is a weekday in May and Scheifele is sitting on the eleventh floor of an office in the cafeteria, a white long-sleeved shirt pulled tight over bulging arm and shoulder muscles. Hearing that Scheifele was once a player who was weak and easily pushed around is sort of like being told that Captain America was once too scrawny and too frail to enlist in World War II. The fictional Steve Rogers received injections of a super-serum to become Captain America, a near-perfect human with super strength, stamina and intelligence. Scheifele developed those same assets, but he got them the hard way.

"Just passion. I'm very, very, very competitive," said Scheifele. "It's pretty much that winning satisfies me. I don't want to lose. So if I pick up a badminton racquet and play you, and you beat me, you're not beating me again. So if you go and train for an hour that day, I'm training for seven hours so that next time I'm beating you."

In a few days, he will represent Canada at the Ice Hockey World Championship in Cologne, Germany, and Paris, France. But on this day, the Winnipeg Jets centre is talking about trying to conquer the world on an individual level. Scheifele, who just turned twenty-four years old, says he wants to be better than Crosby, who just won his third Stanley Cup, and better than McDavid, who just won the Art Ross Trophy (he would win another in 2017–18) and is about to be named league MVP. Four other players finished ahead of Scheifele in the NHL scoring race in 2016–17. He wants to be better than them too.

It's not just lip service. A day earlier, he was on the ice working with skills coach Adam Oates. That was after he spent the morning training with high-performance coach and former NHLer Gary Roberts. When Scheifele's not on the ice or in the gym, the self-professed "hockey nerd" is watching hockey highlights and picking apart subtleties of the game that might give him even the slightest advantage.

"I want to be the best," said Scheifele. "I'm not satisfied with just being in the NHL. I wanted to be a second-line centre in Winnipeg, then a top-twenty scorer in the league, then the top ten, so obviously my goals are higher now. I want to win a scoring title, win a Stanley Cup, win an Art Ross, whatever it is. My goals keep readjusting themselves. But the end goal is to win a Stanley Cup and be MVP of the playoffs."

Scheifele would fall short of that goal in 2018, when the Jets lost to the Vegas Golden Knights in the Western Conference final. But with 14 goals in 17 playoff games, his star continues to burn bright. It's not surprising, considering that a year earlier he finished seventh in league scoring with 32 goals and 82 points in 79 games. And yet, it sort of is when you consider the long road he took to even getting to the NHL.

It's a lesson to any kid who gets cut from a team or is told he is too weak, too slow, too average to be great. Scheifele heard it all and he turned it into motivation. He wasn't the most naturally talented; he was the kid who everyone doubted had decided at an early age to be the most committed and hardest working. He was the rookie who took shots until his fingers bled from the blisters and who insisted on drinking root beer instead of alcohol at an initiation party. Today, it's finally paying off. The late bloomer has blossomed.

> He's like a sponge. Right from age seven when he first started playing, he's been a student of the game who's obsessed. He just loves to learn and loves to hear stories and find anecdotes of what makes players better. If he can instill that in his game and pass it onto others, he'll do that.
>
> **— BRAD SCHEIFELE**

"It's a real learning curve. It doesn't happen overnight. It takes time, right?" said Mark's dad, Brad. "The sky's the limit for every player, but it's nice to see that his game is coming along. It's been a beautiful ride for Mark. When you look at the players who were taken in his draft, Mark has pretty much been number one."

THAT SCHEIFELE TOOK THE LONG ROAD TO THE NHL ISN'T surprising. Travelling long distances is in his blood. For years, Mark's father spent nearly every day on the road, driving a motor coach for a tour bus company he co-owned out of Kitchener, Ontario. During the week, he used to travel everywhere, from New England and the Finger Lakes in central New York to Florida and Branson, Missouri.

Having a father who spent hours upon hours travelling sent a subconscious message to Mark that there are no shortcuts in life. The route from point A to point B is filled with twists and turns and is subject to whatever obstacles the highway throws at you. For Mark, whose career included several detours, it was like that with hockey.

From an early age, he seemed to grasp the idea that you weren't going to get anywhere in life without working for it. Growing up, he played every sport imaginable. His parents had two rules: you could only play two sports per year and once you started a sport, you couldn't quit until the end of the season. In school, Scheifele played everything, including basketball, volleyball and track. When he was in the fourth grade, he was named Athlete of the Year at Grand River Collegiate Institute. "My brother was in grade six at the time," said Scheifele. "That kind of made him mad."

Was he a natural? Yes and no. "I honestly have a natural skill at most things, but I would try pretty hard at it," said Scheifele. Hockey was the passion, though. He didn't just watch hockey games, he watched individual players, studying what made them so successful. He geeked out on the game. He could tell you not only which way a player shot, but also which stick he used and what the curve pattern looked like and how flexible the shaft was.

Despite their son's passion, Scheifele's parents tried to make hockey fun. They never talked about making the NHL or getting a college scholarship or even playing major junior. There was no end goal aside from having fun. "You just wanted them to enjoy what they were doing without putting pressure on them," said Brad Scheifele. "I used to say that whenever they played a rep sport, it was like work because they would be on the ice for five days a week or more. So whenever they had a chance to play pond hockey on an outdoor rink, it was nice to have that available to us."

Stanley Park, in Kitchener, Ontario, where the tennis courts were converted into an outdoor rink in the winter, is just around the corner from where Scheifele grew up. All winter long, he and his brother would walk over and play for hours. In the summer, their street was quiet enough that they could skate around on their rollerblades and play street hockey games without fear of passing cars. Mark, who loved the Detroit Red Wings, always pretended he was Steve Yzerman. His brother was Nicklas Lidström. Or sometimes they were just two goons having a good time. "Yeah, well, realistically I would never be able to beat

Mark Scheifele plays for the Kitchener Jr. Rangers. The Rangers weren't a strong team and won only one tournament. Photo courtesy of the Scheifele family

him because he's two years older than me and two years stronger than me, but I would always try my hardest," said Scheifele. "He would push me down; I would get back up. Obviously we ended in fights a good amount of time, but it was just brotherly love."

Scheifele's parents might not have wanted to put too much stock into their son's hockey career, but Scheifele had other

9

ideas. He was the one, at seven years old, who found out that there would be tryouts for a travel team. And he was the one telling his parents—not the other way around—of the importance of being prepared. His brother joked that he and his sister must have "gotten the lazy genes, where Mark was always keen, always telling you that you have to leave way in advance to get to practice. That was continuous with whatever he was doing."

Scheifele grew up watching Kitchener Rangers games and played for the Jr. Rangers. Photo courtesy of the Scheifele family

Scheifele sounds like a motivational speaker when he talks about his approach to athletics. "You don't play hockey," he said. "You invest in yourself by doing everything possible to be successful." Each year, he tried to find a different regimen to incorporate into his training. One summer, it was his shot. The next, his skating. Slowly he would add to his entire package, getting faster, stronger, smarter, more dominant in each skill. "The road never ends," he said. "Each year there was something that he was going to grab a hold of," said Brad. "I think that learning curve was never-ending, because he knows that you never know everything. It's a fine-tuning kind of thing for him."

Scheifele scored 40 goals and 79 points in 49 games in his minor midget year for the Kitchener Jr. Rangers. But he didn't play in a particularly competitive league. The tournaments his team entered were not against elite competition, so the numbers he was putting up didn't overly impress scouts. Plus, Scheifele wasn't much to look at back then. "I was tall and skinny and played on a pretty weak team in Kitchener so we didn't get a whole lot of exposure," said Scheifele. "We only won one tournament, but it was kind of like a B-level tournament. I don't even think I was on scouts' radar, to be honest."

The Saginaw Spirit selected Scheifele in the seventh round of the OHL draft. At the training camp, he and Vincent Trocheck, who later made the NHL with the Florida Panthers, were trying out for the final spot on the team. Trocheck had been selected twenty-fourth overall. Scheifele and Trocheck tied for first in scoring during the intra-squad games. "Obviously they cut me," said Scheifele. "Said, 'Get stronger,' all that jazz."

Even so, Scheifele wasn't sure the OHL was the right way to go. He had grown up going to Kitchener Rangers games, had watched Derek Roy win a Memorial Cup, had dreamed of doing the same. But after Saginaw cut him, the OHL no longer looked like a real option. College hockey seemed like a better fit for a player who was still growing into his frame. Several schools had shown interest in him. He had even visited Cornell University, where he verbally committed. "I was pretty keen on going there. I was like, 'This is my route.'"

Scheifele was still another year from enrolment, so the decision was where he was going to spend the next season. Initially, the plan was to return to the Kitchener Jr. Rangers for his midget year. But then he got a call from Todd Hoffman. Hoffman, who had coached Scheifele during his OHL draft year, was going to be coaching the Kitchener Dutchmen Junior B team and wanted Scheifele on the team. Hoffman was a more pro-style coach. His son Mike played for the Ottawa Senators, so he had an idea of what Scheifele needed to do to get to the next level. "Having seen his son go through it, he had a better understanding of the draft, all that kind of stuff," said Scheifele.

Still, playing Junior B didn't look like it was going to be a good fit for Scheifele. Junior B level is not a young man's league. The players are typically a lot older and more physically mature. Scheifele wanted to develop—not sit on the bench. "[Mark and his parents] had gone and watched the Junior B level of play in Kitchener. And they hemmed and hawed, because anytime they went and watched that team play it was always the older guys getting ice time," said Hoffman. "So I had to really talk up the program and how I coached. I promised them from day one that he's going to play and he's going to develop. And that's what he did."

Everyone else is such a phenom, but that kid just worked his ass off. He would be on the ice for an hour before practice just shooting pucks. I'd get to the rink and be like, 'Oh shit, he's already been there for thirty minutes.' We didn't have a scheduled workout, but he'd be working with our personal trainer before and after practice. He always wanted to get better. To go from playing Junior B for the Dutchmen to the Barrie Colts and then the NHL in a six-year span is incredible.

— RYAN CLARKSON,
former teammate

RYAN CLARKSON DOESN'T KNOW IF HE SHOULD TELL THIS story. It's not that it's embarrassing. It's just that you know how everyone says what happens in Vegas is supposed to stay in Vegas? Well, what happens at a Rookie Party is supposed to stay at the Rookie Party. But in this case, he will make an exception. Midway through Scheifele's rookie year with the Kitchener Dutchmen, everyone met at teammate Paul Sergi's place in Waterloo for what was framed as a night of team bonding, but was also an excuse to get the first-year players pretty drunk.

Scheifele was not just a rookie. He was an extremely under-aged rookie. And while some sixteen-year-olds would not have thought twice about doing something like drinking beer, Scheifele wasn't like most sixteen-year-olds. At the same time, he didn't want to seem like he wasn't a team player. So he came up with a compromise. "Hey Clarkie," he asked real quietly, when no one was around, "do you think it's all right if I drink root beer?"

If it had been anyone else, Clarkson might have used the moment to embarrass the kid in front of his teammates or maybe used it as a chance to get him even drunker. But Scheifele wasn't anyone else. By the time of the rookie party, he was already the leading scorer and best player on the team. He was clearly headed on a path to the NHL. But more than that, he was someone the veterans liked and respected.

"It was funny, because I usually give it pretty hard to the rookies in the first year," said Clarkson. "I got it bad, too, when I was a rookie. Scheife's the only kid that I let drink straight root beer. Scheife was just such a respectful kid. It's not like he came to me and said, 'I'm drinking root beer.' He asked me politely. What am I going to say? 'No'? Like he's the nicest kid on the planet. I'm like, 'Sure man,' because you knew he was going to make the NHL for sure. If he didn't want to drink, then he doesn't have to drink."

Still, the first time Scheifele arrived at tryouts, it wasn't apparent that he was going to be in the NHL much less lead the Kitchener Dutchmen in scoring. Scheifele didn't even think he was good enough to make the team. It wasn't because he was rail thin or that his skating was sloppy. It was that he still didn't really know how good he was. He didn't grow up being told he was this or that. When he came to the Kitchener Dutchmen, he had just been cut from the Saginaw Spirit after being picked in the seventh round of the OHL draft. His confidence was shot.

"The first time I met him was on the ice," said Clarkson. "I was one of the better players that year coming in and I remember him coming to me and saying, 'Hey Clarkie, do you think I'm going to make the fourth line? Do you think I can make the team?'" In the beginning, Scheifele didn't look special against players who were bigger and physically more mature than him, partly because he was still growing into his body. But the bigger reason was that he was so humble. A rookie's place on most hockey teams is to defer to the veterans. But by the second month of the season, he started to separate himself from everyone else.

"He was a little shy at the time," said Derek Schoenmakers. "But what stood out was that he was a gamer back then. He literally lived and breathed hockey every second of the day. We used to go to his house after practice or it would be the summer and we'd go to the gym for two hours, go home and he'd be wanting to shoot pucks for another two hours after that, to the point where your hands would be ripping apart and he's saying, 'C'mon, one more puck.' That kind of thing. He just lived and breathed hockey. There was no doubt about what he wanted to do. First guy on and last guy off. He loved being at the rink. That's what stood out the most. Obviously, he was an all-world talent."

When he wasn't practising at the rink or working out, Scheifele was at home pounding pucks at his hockey net either by himself or with his teammates. A favourite game was "horse," where the first player tries to hit one of the corner posts with a shot and if he's successful, the next player has to replicate the same shot. If he misses, he gets a letter. The game continues until one of the players has spelled "horse." Or sometimes they would go "around the world" and take turns trying to hit each of the four corner posts and crossbar in succession. "His net was honestly disfigured," said Schoenmakers. "It didn't even look like a net. Posts were curving every which way. It was in shambles."

Scheifele finished the season with 18 goals and 55 points in 51 games. His linemate Clarkson had 27 goals and 43 points. "I was lucky to play with him," said Clarkson. "I can attest that a lot of my goals were because of him. I like to shoot a lot and he was more of a playmaker back then. You can see that he can definitely shoot the puck, but he was always looking to pass first. He set me up a bunch of times, for sure." In the playoffs, Kitchener lost in the first round to Brantford, a team that Clarkson said was "stacked with guys from the OHL."

"We didn't have a deep team or anything like that by any means," said Clarkson. "It was pretty much me and him and our goalie. I remember the playoffs—me and Scheife were playing together and the game we lost 7–5 in Brantford, I believe I scored a hat trick and Scheife had four or five points." Although the season ended earlier than anyone wanted, Scheifele had put himself back on the map. And he did it through perseverance and hard work.

"I honestly believe he wouldn't be where he is today had he not played that year of Junior B," said Hoffman. "I always say, it's not a sprint, it's a marathon. If you've got the aspirations to be an elite player and play in the National Hockey League, like he always had, just be patient. Everything's going to work out at the end of the day if you continue to do the little things on and off the ice the right way. Just look at him today."

DALE HAWERCHUK IS A HALL OF FAME FORWARD WHO scored 1,409 points in 1,188 games during a sixteen-year NHL career. Once he retired, he spent the first few years raising horses in Hockley Valley, Ontario, until one day he "woke up and realized that [he] really missed the game" and got into coaching. In 2010, Hawerchuk had been running a Junior A team in Orangeville when Barrie Colts owner Howie Campbell called and asked if he wanted to take over coaching the team.

It was an offer that came with some serious strings attached. The Colts had just lost in the OHL championship after long-time head coach Marty Williamson suddenly resigned and took a job with the Niagara IceDogs. He wasn't the only one leaving. Alex Pietrangelo, Kyle Clifford, T.J. Brodie and Alex Burmistrov were heading to the NHL, while the team's top-three scorers were also turning pro. Like it or not, the Colts were heading toward a rebuild. The problem was that in a quest for a Memorial Cup, they had given up many of their top prospects and had no one to rebuild around.

So Hawerchuk turned to Scheifele, a Junior B player who a year earlier had been passed up 133 times in the draft because he moved slowly and didn't look like he could handle playing against men. "I had a discussion with Dale Hawerchuk and he said, 'Do you think this kid can play in the league?'" said Hoffman. "And I said, 'He'll come in at the beginning of the year and be a fourth-line guy, but I promise you by Christmas or January, he'll be pushing for a top-six player. He's a real strong player today and he'll get even better, because he wants to be the best. He's that type of kid.'"

But that's not what Hawerchuk saw when he first scouted Scheifele. Watching him play in the Cottage Cup tournament in Huntsville, Ontario, Hawerchuk saw a lanky kid whose skating wasn't exactly fluid. But there was something about the way Scheifele moved around the ice that intrigued Hawerchuk. He wasn't the fastest, but he was rarely out of position. It was like he had an innate knowledge of where the puck was going to be and how to go and get it.

Plus, he had size—and an NHL-calibre release that couldn't be taught. "I just saw instincts," said Hawerchuk. "I saw the routes he was taking away from the puck. He wasn't the greatest skater when I first saw him, but you saw all this good stuff. And then you meet him, and you see he's only going to get better."

Finding Scheifele was the easy part. Getting him to Barrie was a bit more difficult. Scheifele had verbally committed to Cornell University and was planning to spend the season playing

Junior A hockey for the Huntsville Otters before enrolling in college the following year. Well, that was what he had told the Saginaw Spirit. The word around the league was that Scheifele would have no problem playing closer to home, if a team like the Kitchener Rangers were to trade for him.

Before that could happen, Barrie swooped in and acquired his rights from Saginaw. On September 8, 2010, the Colts traded over-age goalie Mavric Parks for Scheifele and a second-round pick in 2013. "When we made the trade, I said to Dale to give it a couple of days and we'll get a call from Kitchener," said Colts general manager Jason Ford, who at the time was the team's assistant GM. "Sure enough, a couple of days passed and we got a call from Kitchener. But we weren't going to trade him."

Instead, after the Cottage Cup ended, the Colts invited Scheifele and his parents to stop by Barrie on their drive back from Huntsville to Kitchener and made their pitch. "I was going to play in Huntsville, actually, because the Huntsville Otters were a Junior A team and they were hosting the RBC Cup and they were trying to load it up. As soon as I left [Barrie], I was like 'I want to play here,'" said Scheifele. "Dale wowed me."

Barrie is a two-hour drive from Kitchener. But what the Colts lacked in geographic proximity, the team made up for by selling Scheifele on its proximity to the NHL. The team was rebuilding and Scheifele would have an opportunity to play more minutes than most rookies usually get. "We also offered him the biggest education package you could get," said Ford.

It was the prospect of playing top-line minutes that meant more to Scheifele. Hawerchuk didn't make any promises. He told Scheifele that nothing would be given to him. This wasn't Junior B. He would have to improve his skating, would have to get stronger and be more responsible defensively. But, as Hawerchuk said, "If you come in here and work hard and you listen to me, I'll get you places." To a workhorse like Scheifele, that was as good as a promise. Said Ford: "[Mark and his parents] thought about it for a day or two and then said, 'Yeah, let's do this.'"

As promised, Scheifele was given a chance to play on the top line. But it came with a cost. Barrie was awful. "I got to go to a team where I got lots of ice time. I got lots of opportunity," said Scheifele. "We had an unbelievable group of guys who all wanted to push each other. We knew our team wasn't great, but we were all going to work hard, whether it was in the gym or on the ice. We would be down 7–1 and no chance against the good teams, but we would battle and be blocking shots until the final second. It was pride. In our minds we didn't want to be embarrassed."

"He really did pay his dues," said Hawerchuk. "A lot of people would say, 'Oh man, the Colts are going to be bad for a while.'" In Hawerchuk, Scheifele had a coach who tapped into his inner hockey nerd. As a former top scorer, he showed Scheifele the black arts of the game, things like how to purposely get lost in the offensive zone to get open for a scoring chance or why you should practise shooting pucks with your head down.

"Everything he said was magnified, because it was Dale Hawerchuk saying it," said Scheifele. "That first year for me—him teaching me little skills, him being on the ice with me each and every day—was huge for my development because it got me to think a different way. It got me to think about the game in new ways and in practice. That was a huge stepping stone for me."

The Colts still struggled and finished with the worst record. But Scheifele was the team's lone bright spot, finishing second in rookie scoring with 75 points in 66 games, behind only Sarnia's Nail Yakupov. By the end of the year, the late bloomer who got cut from his junior team was now considered a first-round prospect.

"It took him a while to get the hang of things, but you look at his game-to-game, I think he had 75 points that year and I'm going to say that 45 of them came after Christmas," said Ford. "If

Yakupov wasn't in the league, [Scheifele] would have won rookie of the year easily. And then he just kept moving up the draft rankings. He worked himself up from being on nobody's NHL radar to by the end of the year almost every team thinking he was a first-rounder."

A year earlier, there were questions regarding Scheifele's skating and strength. Now, the questions were about how this kid could get so good in such a short time. "When you meet Mark, you realize that he's only going to get better because his passion for the game is so strong," said Hawerchuk. "I don't know what to call it, but if you're trying to find the right attitude for a hockey player, he's that guy. He's ultra-competitive with everything. When Winnipeg were thinking about drafting him, they called me after the interview and said, 'Is this kid for real?'"

"MAKE THE SHOW." THAT'S WHAT THEY USED TO SAY TO MOTIVATE EACH other when they were tired. If you don't do fifty push-ups, you're not going to make the show. If you don't take one hundred shots, you're not going to make the show. It didn't matter what it was. For Scheifele and Ekblad, everything revolved around making the show—playing in the NHL.

If Scheifele had been a late bloomer, then Ekblad, who was the OHL's first overall pick in 2011, was the exact opposite. But while their paths looked different, their work ethic was the same. In drills, Ekblad sought out Scheifele— two alpha dogs fighting over the same bone. "I didn't find out until halfway through the year. I was like, 'Hey, let's go against each other,'" Scheifele said to Ekblad. "He's like, 'I've been doing it the whole year.' I didn't even realize it. But it made sense. If you want to challenge yourself, if you want to be the best, then you have to go against the best."

ON MAY 31, 2011, THE ATLANTA THRASHERS WERE SOLD TO True North Sports & Entertainment and relocated to Winnipeg. Two weeks later, Kevin Cheveldayoff was hired as the team's new general manager. The Jets weren't an expansion team. They were inheriting a decent roster consisting of Blake Wheeler, Dustin Byfuglien, Andrew Ladd, Evander Kane and Bryan Little. But they had made the post-season only once in their eleven-year history and had not won a single playoff game during that time. A rebuild was necessary. The way to do that was by finding a franchise player with the seventh overall pick in the NHL Entry Draft.

It was an important pick. Cheveldayoff knew whoever the Jets selected would forever be tied to version 2.0 of the Jets. At the same time, he wasn't necessarily looking for someone to plaster on billboards or help sell tickets. He just wanted someone with character, who could grow and develop with the team, and make a long-term impact. In some ways, they were looking for a late bloomer.

"I think that the biggest thing we had going for us was when I sat down with [owners] Mark Chipman and David Thomson about the direction of the team when we first took over, we said this isn't going to be a short-term fix type of thing," said Cheveldayoff. "We're going to draft and we're going to develop and by drafting we have to be prepared to send players back to junior if they are physically not ready. Their talents are probably there, but they're physically not. One thing we stressed right from the moment that we took over is that this was going to be our draft list. It wasn't going to be a list of what would have consensus potentially throughout the National Hockey League by the different pundits or the different reporting agencies or anything like that. As we continued to go through the process, Mark's name kept coming up."

Scheifele was still flying a bit under the radar at the time. *The Hockey News* had him forty-first overall in their pre-draft rankings, calling him an "interesting case study" because he had put up big-time points—albeit on the worst team in the OHL. "He wasn't that prototypical, you know, exceptional kid that was petitioning the OHL to play at the elite level at a super young age," said Cheveldayoff. "He took different steps along the way, including going to Barrie and having a very good first year and getting on everyone's radar."

Once they picked Scheifele, the bigger question became what to do with him. In his first training camp, he had played well enough to stick with the team. But Hawerchuk convinced the Jets to send him back. It wasn't for selfish reasons. Hawerchuk had scored 183 points in his final year of junior before jumping to the NHL and scoring 103 points as a rookie with the Jets. That wasn't a fluke, he said. You can't expect to score 100 points in the NHL if you haven't first learned how to score 100 points in the level below.

"The whole premise on that was to develop dominance," said Hawerchuk. "I said, 'Look, you want him to be dominant in the NHL, he's got to learn how to do it here first, because if he doesn't do it here he's not going to understand how to do it against men all the time. He needs to learn how to be dominant, and it takes success and it takes a mindset and then when you have success, your mind says, 'Oh yeah, I can be that dominant guy.' When you become dominant at a level, you learn to kick it in gear all the time."

The following season, the Colts drafted Ekblad with the first overall pick and Barrie went from bottom feeder to legitimate contender. Scheifele and Ekblad were perfect for each other, constantly raising and re-raising the bar. Scheifele scored 63 points in 47 games in 2011–12. The next year, with the NHL lockout cancelling the first three months of the season, he spent a third year in Barrie, scoring 79 points in 45 games.

"I definitely wasn't ready for it yet," Scheifele said of waiting two years before playing in the NHL. "I definitely had some growth I needed to do. I kept working at my game, working at my game, inside and out, each year I grew more and more, both physically and mentally; that's just the person I am."

"It just really underscores that when Mark Scheifele was physically ready to play, he blossomed," said Cheveldayoff. "You really can't underestimate the work that Mark put in. He invests in himself, whether it's physically or nutritionally, and he's a hockey nut. He literally loves the game. Watches it, dissects it, talks about it, laughs about it, gets angry at it. It's a real pleasure to have players like that in the league."

In 2013, long-time coach Paul Maurice was in between coaching jobs and working as a TV analyst for TSN in Canada. During one segment, a question was posed: "Is Mark Scheifele a bust?" At the time, Scheifele had twice been returned to junior and was on his way to an average rookie season with the Jets in which he scored 13 goals and 34 points in 63 games. For a player who had been drafted seventh overall, the fans were already giving up on him before his career had a chance to take off.

"I remember thinking, 'He's going back to play junior because he's supposed to,'" said Maurice. "The pressure these guys are under to come in at eighteen, nineteen, and be great is huge. And if they're not, it's 'What's going on here?' But Mark has had a very consistent level of progress. And boom, he gets 82 points and it's a breakout year, but if you watched, he just got better every day. That's been the story of his whole career."

CALGARY FLAMES
» № 13 «

POSITION	LEFT WING
SHOOTS	RIGHT
HEIGHT	5'9"
WEIGHT	157 LB
BORN	AUGUST 13, 1993
BIRTHPLACE	SALEM, NJ, USA
DRAFT	2011 CGY, 4TH RD, 13TH PK (104TH OVERALL)

Johnny Gaudreau (left) sprints for the puck in a 2017 game against the Maple Leafs. The Canadian Press/Nathan Denette

I T STARTED WITH CANDY. SKITTLES, TO BE EXACT. SOME kids first learn to skate by putting their hands on the seat of a chair and pushing it around the ice. Others simply grab hold of their mom or dad's hands for balance and away they go. Johnny Gaudreau got started by literally chasing after a sugar high. Forget a chair or his parents' hands. For a kid with a mighty big sweet tooth, what got him up and moving were the candies his dad scattered on the ice.

Johnny was eighteen months old when his dad first put him on skates. Initially, Johnny sat in one spot and refused to move. "I don't think he's going to make it here," Guy Gaudreau said to his wife. She replied, "Why don't we see once he has his diapers off?" The next time out, Johnny's dad came prepared with a bag of Skittles. He put Johnny on the ice and then put one of the candies just out of reach of his son. At first, Johnny crawled to it on his hands and knees. *Hmm*, his dad thought, *this isn't quite working*.

Other kids were also on the ice learning how to skate. So Guy Gaudreau, who was the hockey director at Hollydell Ice Arena in Sewell, New Jersey, poured the entire bag into his hand and with a sweeping motion scattered the brightly coloured candies like chicken feed all over the ice. Johnny still crawled. But this time the other kids—who could skate and had just discovered that the ice was littered with sweet candy—were beating him to the Skittles. So Johnny eventually did what Charles Darwin had

Johnny GAUDREAU

predicted prehistoric sea creatures had done so many years and evolutions ago: he got up on his feet and tried to walk.

"After a couple of months, I'd start skating around the other kids," said Gaudreau. "It's a pretty unique story." That's the story of how Gaudreau learned to skate. The story of how he got to the NHL is a bit more complicated. It involves a father-coach-counsellor who should have been an NHLer if he were two inches taller,

Johnny Gaudreau learns to skate. Photo courtesy of the Gaudreau family

a college coach who emphasized skill over size and strength, and countless other coaches, scouts and general managers who believed in him. But mostly it involves rejection—lots and lots of rejection.

After all, Skittles might coax you onto the ice, but they can't make you taller. While Gaudreau's sweet tooth got bigger over the years ("When it came time to cleaning my room, the Skittles were huge," he said. "Every Christmas or any holiday, I'd get bags of them as presents."), his body never really caught up to his peers'. He was always the smallest player on every team he played on. When he played in the United States Hockey League (USHL), a teammate jokingly made him a stepstool so he could get his equipment off the top shelf in the dressing room. He was so small that he was constantly mistaken for the stick boy or someone's younger brother, and routinely got cut from teams before even stepping on the ice.

"There were many times when I had to talk him off the ledge," said Guy Gaudreau. "Telling him, 'It's okay, just have fun and play. Good things will happen. You're going to be a late bloomer like me.' He never bought into all that stuff. It was hard for him." It was frustrating and infuriating, but it was part of what made Gaudreau so great. Two things can happen when you face adversity: you can pout and accept that the world is conspiring against you, or you can adapt and evolve. Gaudreau chose the latter. He accepted that he was never going to be the tallest or strongest, so he attempted to use his size to his advantage. His journey from being passed up for the World Junior Championship team to becoming Johnny Hockey involves hockey smarts and hours of bag skates, a junior coach who gave him a chip on his shoulder and a college coach who believed undersized players had a place in the sport.

But mostly, it came from Gaudreau deciding that if he wanted to get more Skittles than the bigger kids, he was going to have to get up off his hands and knees and skate for them. "I definitely got cut from festival teams. I mean, I don't know if I should say I should have been put on that team. Everyone has their own opinions. But I personally thought I should have made teams. That's part of the game. Sometimes you get cut and it shows you a little of adversity and makes you a better player. Maybe it's good that I got cut."

YOU CANNOT TELL THE STORY OF HOW JOHNNY GAUDREAU got to the NHL without first telling the story of why his father did not get to the NHL. Guy Gaudreau was born on a dairy farm in Beebe Plain, Vermont, a small town of about five hundred that extends into Stanstead, Quebec. There's no gas station. But growing up, Guy had a backyard rink to skate on every winter.

Like his two sons, he was a natural athlete growing up. It didn't matter what the sport was, Guy would excel at it. As a soccer player, he led North Country Union High to back-to-back state championships and graduated as the school's all-time scoring leader. He then enrolled at Norwich University, where as a senior he was named to the All–New England team and graduated as the school's all-time scoring leader. But hockey was his passion. His high school didn't get a hockey team until his second year, but Gaudreau quickly turned them into a state powerhouse, scoring 118 goals in his three years and leading the school to a 15–0 record and a berth in the state final as a senior. The success continued at Norwich University, where he was the team's MVP as a senior and graduated in the top five in scoring with 88 goals and 144 points. "Guy is a natural athlete," said Mike Green, a family friend. "There's nothing surprising that his boys are terrific athletes too."

I knew that he loved the game. His passion for the game was probably more than I've ever seen and his competitive drive was more than I've ever seen. I've coached a lot of years and coached a lot of kids and I don't know if I know anybody who loves the game as much as him. He's happiest when he's on the ice, whether it's a practice or a power skating class or a big game or scrimmage.

— **GUY GAUDREAU**

In 2017, Guy Gaudreau became the first student athlete to be inducted into the Vermont Sports Hall of Fame. By all accounts, he probably should have played in the NHL or at the very least should have played pro somewhere. But no matter how skilled he was or how fast he could skate, it took a long time for the hockey world to catch up to forwards who were so small that they could barely see over the boards. "I was always considered a small hockey player, a small athlete," said Guy. "Plus, I was brought up on a dairy farm in Vermont, so I didn't have a lot of opportunities to be showcased or to be seen. I think

I lost out on a lot there. If I had more opportunities, I might have had more success with the game."

Instead, Guy went into the family business. By then, his father had set up a five hundred–acre spring water facility and Guy was charged with expanding the company and setting up distribution in South Jersey. It didn't last. His heart was still in hockey. When Hollydell Ice Arena was built about seven years later, Guy volunteered his time, teaching learn-to-skate clinics and running the men's league. There was always something new to be done and Gaudreau always seemed to be the first one putting up his hand to do it, to the point where it was becoming a full-time job for him. So he figured why not make it official? Gaudreau sold his part of the water business and went into the ice business. "This fell into what I really like to do," Guy Gaudreau said of running a hockey rink. "It was a lot more fun than peddling water around and having people destroy your vans and people not showing up for work when they were supposed to."

For Johnny and his younger brother Matt, having a dad who ran a hockey rink was better than having a dad who played in the NHL. Guy not only knew the game, but he was around to teach it. And when he was too busy to play, Johnny and his brother and their friends were welcome to hop on the ice. "It was great for me. I had ice time whenever I wanted it," said Johnny. "I played for three or four different teams, was on the ice for every single practice. I was on the ice for four hours at a time. I think it helped me get to where I am today."

Hollydell Arena has two ice rinks, a snack bar and an arcade filled with eighties-style video games. It's Chuck E. Cheese's, except a lot colder. Upstairs, where one of the offices has been transformed into a sort of thrift store for hockey players, is undoubtedly the coolest. Practice jerseys in every imaginable colour are hanging from hooks. Equipment in all shapes and sizes is scattered on the tops of lockers and overflowing out of bins. On any given night, Guy Gaudreau is the behind-the-scenes stylist. A team needs a sub? "Here, grab this red jersey." A player forgot his gloves? "Pick a pair from the pile and go. C'mon, get out there, there's hockey to be played."

"I'm a school teacher and I admire all the people who aren't above doing whatever needs to get done," said Mike Green, who has known Guy since Green signed his son up to play hockey and was roped in by the full-of-energy rink manager to help coach. "Guy is in charge of hockey operations, but he's also the guy who made sure that the locker rooms were clean by cleaning them himself. If you've ever met his wife, Jane, she is also like that."

Everyone around Guy Gaudreau is like that. His enthusiasm is irresistible. With Guy, you can't say no. So Green learned that sometimes it's best to arrive to the rink incognito. After all, a one-hour practice for your son can turn into a three-hour night if one of the men's teams is short a player and Guy catches you walking around. "You get there and there's a game going on and Guy would say, 'We need you for this men's league game!' And you're like, 'I can't, my equipment's at home, another time.'"

Guy's response: "Don't worry. There's stuff upstairs!" That's Guy. He's a hockey lifer. He lives it, breathes it and has such an infectious personality that he makes you want to live it and breathe it also. He coaches multiple teams, plays on multiple teams and is involved in every facet of the game, from creating the skills programs to organizing the men's leagues to driving the Zamboni. Up until 2017—long after both his sons had moved on to college—he was the head coach of Gloucester Catholic, where both Johnny and Matthew had gone to school. "He still plays in the alumni game for my high school," said Green. "And he didn't even go to my high school."

The first time Green met Johnny Gaudreau's dad, Guy took a look at Green's beat-up skates and concluded he was the person to help coach the kids' hockey team. They were beat up just enough for him to trust that Green had been a good player. "Whenever he was looking for guys to coach, he used to say that the guy who came in with new skates was the one he was always worried about," said Green. "The guys who had skates like mine used to play some place."

Coaching was easy with a player like Johnny Gaudreau. He was a natural, a little water bug who whirled around the ice as though he were running on batteries. He never wanted to come off the ice after a shift, never wanted to leave the rink. Growing up, Gaudreau played two years above his age level, but he played on other teams too—whoever needed a sub, just about every team imaginable that needed a sub. That still wasn't enough for him. The problem was that there wasn't a travel team for kids that young, so Gaudreau's dad and Mike Green came up with an idea: how about a "limited travel" team that would get the parents and kids an introduction to what the next few years would hold?

The word "limited," however, was debatable. "We came up with this schedule and the parents were looking at it like, 'Well gee, this is a lot more than we anticipated,'" said Green. "We're playing hockey every weekend. We're going to Pennsylvania and northern New Jersey. And we're like, 'But it's limited travel!' Guy's ability to get us on the ice for different things, especially the way

Johnny Gaudreau plays for Gloucester Catholic High. Photo courtesy of the Gaudreau family

he ran practices, was uncanny. He would run a lot of three-on-three. There was so much joy. My memories were of John never wanting to leave the ice."

Guy Gaudreau is 5-foot-8. His wife Jane is even shorter. So Johnny and Matthew knew early on that the growth spurt that other kids had already received probably wasn't ever going to come. They were always going to be the smallest players on their hockey teams, the kids who are inevitably put in the front row on picture day. At times, it was a frustrating plight. Had Gaudreau been just a little taller, just a couple of inches really, he might have been looked at differently, might not have had to jump over so many hurdles and deal with so much rejection.

Johnny Gaudreau was always the smallest player on every team he played for—but he could skate like no one else. Photo courtesy of the Gaudreau family

Even his father believed Johnny would hit a wall someday—the same wall that had put a stop to his own dreams. "It's tough for a parent when your son wants to be a Division-1 hockey player and a pro hockey player and you know he's not going to be very big," said Guy Gaudreau. "You know they like guys who are 6-foot-1 or taller and there was no way in hell that he was going to be that tall, so it was hard as a parent whenever he got cut from a team."

If Johnny wasn't ever going to be the biggest player, then his father made sure Johnny was going to be the best skater. "He skated the crap out of us when we were younger," said Johnny. "Anytime we lost, the next day the first thirty-five minutes of prac-tice there wouldn't be any pucks. We'd be skating the whole time. By the end of practice when we did get pucks, we'd be too tired to shoot them. Yeah, I hated them. If we lost on the weekend, I dreaded Monday practice. That was just his style. You were going to skate. That helped me out a lot, just being conditioned from skating all the time."

It wasn't just that Johnny skated. It was how he skated. Guy Gaudreau was a big believer that you should skate from the waist down and play hockey from the waist up. It was something he learned while attending one of former NHLer Howie Meeker's summer hockey camps as a kid and the technique stuck with him and made sense, especially as an undersized player who relied heavily on his mobility. "When you skate, your arms, shoulders and upper torso should be quiet," said Guy Gaudreau. In other words, don't swing your arms by your side. Don't pump your shoul-ders like pistons. Instead, let your legs do the work and reserve your arms and hands for stickhandling and manoeuvring.

"If you watch John skate or my other son, Matthew, skate, they do skate from the waist down pretty well, so it gives them an opportunity to shoot and pass and see the rink a little better than when your arms are moving and your head is moving," said Guy Gaudreau. "It helps you succeed, especially if you're a small player."

One thing Guy couldn't teach Johnny was how to think the game. When most kids—or NHL players, for that matter—have the puck behind the net, they skate to try to stuff it into the far side. If they're quick enough, they might beat the goalie and the defencemen and score. Johnny looked at the problem differently. "He'd go behind the net, turn one way and then stop and turn the other way and be able to come out the other side where no one is there and put it in the net," said Guy Gaudreau. "Kids wouldn't even think about that. He did things that you can't coach."

And yet at times, he was a player that coaches didn't want. It wasn't because of a lack of skill. As a thirteen-year-old, he tried out and made a festival team that cobbled together the best kids in his district. The next two years, he was cut. It didn't take long for Gaudreau to realize why. The body does a lot of its growing from thirteen to fifteen and while the other kids had become taller and stronger, Gaudreau remained the same size. Gaudreau was deflated. If he wasn't big enough to play on a rep team in New Jersey, what chance did he have at playing in the NHL?

"I remember his first year of bantam; he might have had 93 points in like 35 games and was the highest scorer on the team and he went to a district tournament and got cut," said Guy. "And there's kids making it who I thought weren't even close to his calibre, but they didn't want him because he was so small. I was so mad." Guy never made a stink about it. He's not that type of person. Plus, he didn't want to fight Johnny's battles. Better that his son realize what obstacles were in front of him so that he could figure out a way around them by himself. All Guy did was tell Johnny that if there was something worth fighting for, then he better get back on his hands and knees and crawl for it, one more Skittle at a time.

"If it's meant to be then it's meant to be," said Guy. "You just keep working harder and harder and either it's going to happen or it's not going to happen. But there's a lot of people who were a part of that who now won't look me in the eye. So I got the last laugh."

THE PAIN WAS INTENSE. CRAMPS LIKE HE'D NEVER IMAGINED. GAUDREAU thought his appendix had burst or worse. Eventually, he couldn't take it anymore. "Coach, my stomach is killing me," he said in the middle of practice.

"What's wrong, Johnny? Do you need to go to the hospital or something?"

"I don't know, coach."

So they took him to the team doctor, who asked Gaudreau if he had eaten anything differently. Maybe it was food poisoning. It wasn't. Well, not exactly.

"I find out he's been trying to put on some weight and that he loves chocolate, so he's pounding Nutella right out of the jar," said Dubuque head coach Jim Montgomery. "It was binding him up so bad that he couldn't go to the bathroom."

FIRST IMPRESSIONS ARE ALWAYS THE SAME. SOMEONE TAKES one look at Johnny Gaudreau and automatically assumes he cannot actually be a hockey player. He must be the stick boy or someone's kid brother or a young fan that snuck in the dressing room somehow. No one thinks he belongs on the ice, much less that he can play. The first time Jiri Hudler met Gaudreau was during the Calgary Flames' final trip of the 2013–14 season. "I remember him walking onto the plane and I had no idea it was him," said the 5-foot-10 Hudler, who played on the same forward line as Gaudreau during his rookie season in Calgary. "This kid looks like he was twelve years old—and he still does—so I thought someone from management was bringing their son on the trip. I'm serious. You see the body structure and he's a little guy."

It was like that when Gaudreau joined the Dubuque Fighting Saints in the USHL. The team was an expansion franchise in its first season in the league. So when some of the players saw Gaudreau sitting in the dressing room, they thought this had to be some kind of joke. C'mon now, we know we're an expansion team and expected to pay our dues, but this is the best we can do? "I swear I thought it was someone's little brother," said Shane Sooth. "He could have been in middle school, that's no exaggeration."

And then, of course, came the big reveal: Gaudreau got on the ice and his size wasn't a detriment. If anything, it was an asset. He did things with the puck that as if he was playing a video game using cheat codes. The puck appeared to be taped to his stick. His skates, which he wore so loose that it looked like his feet were going to pop out of them, seemed to be magnetized to the ice. "We had this guy who was 6-foot-5 and 250 pounds and you just see the difference between them and you think to yourself there's no way this kid's going to last," said Sooth. "But you couldn't even touch him. It was ridiculous."

Gaudreau scored the first goal in the Fighting Saints' history and finished fourth in scoring, leading all rookies with 36 goals and 72 points in 60 games. "His ability, his hockey smarts, were off the charts," said Jim Montgomery. "When we did two-on-one drills, I'd let it go an extra rep just to see what he would come up with the next time."

It wasn't just Gaudreau's coach who was doing a double take. Once, an opposing coach had seen Gaudreau and others on the team playing two-touch with a soccer ball in the hallway before a game. After the game, the coach came over to Montgomery and mentioned how sweet it was of him to allow the equipment manager to take part in the practice sessions. He didn't realize that the person he thought was the equipment manager had actually scored all three goals in the game—all on wraparounds.

"Rim it behind the net to Johnny and let him do his thing," Montgomery shouted to the players on the power play. "He's probably the best I've seen behind there," said Montgomery, "and the most dangerous and creative player since Gretzky or maybe Doug Gilmour. He would do these little cutbacks and then stuff it into the open side."

There were two expansion teams that year: Dubuque and the Muskegon Lumberjacks. Neither was supposed to do much. "I know people at the start of the year were saying if you guys challenge for a playoff spot that would be a really good start," said Montgomery. But Dubuque finished first in the Western

36

Conference with a record of 37–14–9 and went on to win the Clark Cup. Gaudreau, who scored 5 goals and 11 points in 11 playoff games, was the major reason for it.

"It was a surprise to everyone. It was really impressive," said Montgomery. "Even in the USHL today, players don't put up numbers like they do in the [Canadian Hockey League (CHL)]. And in the playoffs, he was unbelievable, scoring the big goals at the big moments, being the difference maker and separating us from the teams we were playing against. I remember the game-winning goal in Game 2 of the semifinals. We created a turnover in the neutral zone and Johnny had just come off the bench. He grabbed the puck for a partial breakaway. He was clearly not going to get to the net. The defenceman was angling him off and the goalie was in position. But he dropped his shoulder and got the goalie leaning one way and he put the puck on the short side just under the crossbar. We slowed it down afterwards to see what he was shooting at and maybe two pucks could have fit in where he put it."

It wasn't just that Gaudreau was scoring, it was that he was doing it in a league where the players were bigger than he had ever played against. The USHL is a stepping stone for a lot of players on their way to college. But it's also the last stop for over-agers looking at one last kick at the can. There was one player in the league with 259 penalty minutes. And here was Gaudreau, a player who was so small that Sooth jokingly made him a stool in wood shop—with his nickname "GOO" on it—so he could reach his skates.

"He was basically like a twelve-year-old playing with men, but destroying them," said Sooth. "In the beginning of the year, we got into a line brawl. Johnny was on the bench and I actually got beat up pretty good. But we had two of the toughest guys in the league on our team. Everyone knew if they touched Johnny they would have to go through them."

Gaudreau was fearless. He didn't avoid the danger areas and didn't play scared. Yes, he was tiny. But he never really made it seem like it was a negative because of all the goals he was scoring. "His timing in getting into tough scoring areas was impeccable," said Montgomery. "When we played the most physical team in the league, that's when I knew he had a chance to play in the NHL, because he fought through a lot of hooking and whacking and stuff after the whistle and was our best player."

Still, Montgomery wanted Gaudreau to get bigger. If nothing else, he wanted him to get healthier. "He's got horrible eating habits," said Montgomery, remembering back to when the Fighting Saints held a team barbecue at the start of the season and Gaudreau skipped the salads and went straight for the meat.

"All he puts on his plate are three hamburgers," said Montgomery. "Not even cheese. Just ketchup. My three-year-old is eating the same thing. I never cared about [Gaudreau's] weight. For me, I just cared that he had some muscle definition in and around his joints. At some point, even as elusive as he is, you're going to get clipped and you just want your joints to be strong enough to absorb the odd big hit. You see his frame right now and you see that he has put in the work and that's why he's been able to absorb the hits he has taken at the NHL level. But you don't want a guy like that taking away even a millisecond or second of quickness, because that's worse than putting on five more pounds. Let's put it this way: he was a child and all he would eat would be candy and milkshakes."

Eventually, Gaudreau found a way to put on weight without making himself sick—or actually eating anything. A hockey puck weighs 6 ounces. Stack six of them together and you have 2.25 pounds. Gaudreau knows this because when NHL Central Scouting sent one of its scouts to Dubuque to officially weigh all the draft-eligible players, Gaudreau started stuffing as many pucks into his shorts as possible. It was only a couple of pounds, but when you're as small as he is, every pound counts. Feeling heavier and more confident, Gaudreau stepped on the scale. As he did, a puck dropped out of his shorts and hit the ground. And then another fell. He looked up, smiling. "The guy was like, 'It's okay, I'll give you two extra pounds for trying,'" said Montgomery.

THEY WERE AFRAID HE WAS GOING TO BE OFF THE BOARD. Can you believe it? Gaudreau, who was the smallest player ranked by NHL Central Scouting, was apparently a hot commodity going into the 2011 NHL Entry Draft. Well, lukewarm might be the better adjective. The Calgary Flames wanted him. So did the Bruins— GM Peter Chiarelli was also the owner of the Dubuque Fighting Saints—and the Coyotes and several other teams. It was just a matter of when they were willing to gamble on taking him.

First round? Second round? Third? By the fourth round, Calgary couldn't wait any longer, using the 104th overall pick on a 5-foot-6 and 137-pound winger whom NHL Central Scouting listed as the smallest in the draft—whom the Flames didn't even have on any of their lists.

"'Cloak and dagger' would be a good headline, I guess," said Calgary Flames' director of scouting Tod Button, who asked then-GM Jay Feaster to keep Gaudreau off their scouting lists for fear that word would get out that they were interested in him. "We certainly didn't want to give away the fact that we like Johnny," said Button. "Jay's mantra for that draft was we're going to make our list number 1 to 100 and we're going to go right off the list. So when a guy's taken, we're going to cross him off and pick the next guy on our list. But when we put the numbers up, Johnny should have been in the top twenty on our list. But I also didn't want to rank and rate him—I wanted to have the leeway where if I thought it was the right time we could pick him. And that's how it went. For Johnny, it was purely his size. You sit in the scouts' room and you hear the guy's a good player, but he's just too small. We said the same thing. We were worried about his size too. Nowadays people don't have that concern anymore."

DON'T JUDGE A BOOK BY ITS COVER. THAT'S HOW JERRY YORK, the long-time head coach of Boston College, talks about his experience coaching Gaudreau. Of course, York didn't judge. He's been around far too long, seen too much, to disregard a player just because of his size. Besides, he likes smaller, skilled players. He is, after all, the coach who gave Mike Cammalleri and Brian Gionta a shot, the coach who trained Nathan Gerbe and Ryan Shannon and Cam Atkinson. He's been Papa Smurf to a roster full of mite-sized players.

So when York saw what Gaudreau did at Dubuque in the USHL, he knew Boston College would be a perfect fit. The feeling was mutual. "Boston College is known for their smaller guys and Jerry York did a great job of helping me out," said Gaudreau. "He made me. At Boston College, I realized that my size wasn't a downfall to my game; that I should use it to my advantage. I was playing against men. But guys couldn't hit me if I used my speed and my creativity and made plays. Jerry York is a huge part of why I'm here today."

York might have been a believer from the very start. But Gaudreau's teammates shared the skepticism that has dogged him throughout his career. Gaudreau, whom the Flames had already drafted, showed up to a team meeting in the summer before his freshman season feeling everyone's eyeballs on him. *Not this again,* he thought. "One of the captains we had asked me, 'Is he this good, coach, because he doesn't look big enough for this level,'" said York. "Sometimes you get fooled by the cover of the book."

Once again, Gaudreau proved everyone wrong. He stepped on the ice and the players, who were bigger and better than they had been in the USHL, couldn't touch Gaudreau. He spun around checks, darted in and out of traffic, and electrified everyone with his moves. "From the first practice, you could tell right away that this was a hockey player," said York.

But he still didn't look like a hockey player. York tried to change that. Gaudreau didn't have the body type to stand in the ring with the heavyweights or even the middleweights, but there was no reason why he couldn't add muscle to his tiny frame. That meant introducing him to a place called the weight room. And convincing him that Skittles weren't technically part of the five food groups.

"First and foremost, we tried to impress upon him that off-ice conditioning was going to be as important as his on-ice development," said York. "He used to get so excited when the Zamboni cleaned the ice. He'd say, 'Hey, the ice is all set, coach.' We wanted to try to convince him that there's a weight room too. It's fresh and it's clean and all set for him too. Be excited about that. Be excited about planks and bench presses. The next step was to try to get him off Skittles and more toward protein. Again, we weren't as successful as I wanted. But I think we got him pointed in the right direction."

Gaudreau had a banner year, leading all freshmen in scoring with 21 goals and 44 points in 44 games, winning a national title, and earning MVP honours in both the Hockey East Tournament and the Beanpot Tournament. And yet, they came with an asterisk. During the national championship game against Ferris State, Gaudreau scored a highlight reel goal, kicking the puck up to his stick and turning a defender inside out with a deke before roofing a backhand to put the game out of reach. But on the ESPN broadcast, commentators once again called him "tiny" and said, "He looks about twelve years old."

It was a familiar refrain. Earlier that year, Gaudreau had been cut from the US World Junior Championship team, despite being one of the best college players in the country. "He went to tryouts in December and we fully expected him to make the team—because we had watched him those first four months as a freshman—but then in the selection process they sent him home," said York. "I thought he really took it hard and when he came back to our practice sessions, he was even more determined. I think that kind of got him going, boy. 'If they don't think I'm good enough, I'm going to show them.' So you think about it, the next year he's the best player in the tournament and the year before he can't make it. That really spurred him. That rejection he took in the right way."

The next year, there was no way he was being left off the US team. In fact, on a team that included six first-round draft picks, he was the best player. It was a shock and yet it wasn't. Gaudreau wasn't the only undersized player that year. Rocco Grimaldi, his linemate for part of the tournament, was 5-foot-6. "Obviously [Gaudreau] was going to be on our team," said Phil Housley, who was the head coach of Team USA in 2013. "He was a great player in college and his game continued to grow. I mean, they showed me some video of him before we went on the ice, just to get an understanding of how good he was, but to actually see him live, you could tell that his instincts and hockey IQ were off the charts. I was like, 'This guy's special.' You could tell right away. There was no doubt in my mind. He was a big part of our team. It was just a matter of finding the right people to play with him who would play the game the way he thought."

Gaudreau led the tournament with 7 goals in 7 games and helped the US win gold. "He didn't start out well in the tournament," said Housley. "I think he had some really good looks to score against Russia and Canada, whom we lost to 2–1 and 2–1 in that tournament. But in the next game he scored and then had a hat trick. And then he just took off. I think he just needed to hit the twine to get some confidence. As a player, you're squeezing the stick and waiting for something to happen and he made it happen eventually. You have to look at the level of competition. Canada, I think, had fifteen or sixteen first-rounders. Russia had a really strong team. And he was able to find his way through those teams."

When Gaudreau returned to Boston College, things continued to click for him. He finished the season with 36 goals and 80 points in 40 games—a 2.00 point-per-game pace that made him the highest scorer in the National Collegiate Athletic Association (NCAA) and easily won him the Hobey Baker Award as the NCAA's top player. "That was his motivation. 'I'm going to show these guys that I'm better than they think,'" said York. "He's not just playing in the World Juniors, he's playing the world championship and he was one of the best there too. I watch all our players on TV and you watch Johnny play and it's like, 'Whoa, he's become a high-end, high-end player, I'll tell you, boy.'"

I think the first time I saw John play and thought he had a chance at making it was when he played for the World Juniors. I don't know how he made that team but he made it and he went over to Ufa, Russia, and I'm watching him play against all these first-round draft picks and he's one of the best players on that team. And I'm thinking, "Yeah, maybe he has a chance. He might make it. He might prove me wrong." They won the gold medal and he was the highest scorer on the team and selected to the all-star team and won MVP in three or four games. I'm like, something's not right here, he's playing with J.T. Miller and Seth Jones and Jacob Trouba and guys who are going to make the NHL. And he's on the ice all the time and carrying the team.

— **GUY GAUDREAU**

HE DOESN'T REALLY GO BY JOHNNY OR JOHNNY HOCKEY. DID you know that? To his family and friends and coaches, he is simply John. "Anybody who's known John since he was a baby or growing up, to our friends, his name is John Michael Gaudreau," said Guy

Gaudreau. "He became Johnny when he went to Boston College. Everyone called him Johnny. They would chant, 'John-ny! John-ny!' And it kind of took off from there. And then they started calling him Johnny Hockey."

It wasn't exactly an original nickname. A couple of years earlier, high school quarterback Johnny Manziel had been dubbed "Johnny Football." By Manziel's sophomore season at Texas A&M, he was on his way to winning a Heisman Trophy as the best college player. That same year, with Gaudreau on his way to winning the Hobey Baker Award and electrifying the NCAA with highlight-reel goals, fans started calling him "Johnny Hockey." Whenever he scored a goal at home, the Boston College prep band would play Chuck Berry's "Johnny B. Goode." The nickname took off and soon, it was appearing everywhere. The family got concerned. In 2016, they trademarked "Johnny Hockey" in Canada and the United States. "Someone tried to start 'Johnny Effing Hockey,'" said Guy Gaudreau, purposely leaving out the swear word. "We weren't too pleased with that. We said we better patent this so people can't make T-shirts and stuff with this. We didn't want people using [the name] inappropriately."

Call it one of the downsides of Gaudreau's somewhat unlikely rise to becoming one of the top players of his generation. Back when he was getting cut from festival teams and overlooked by scouts, no one could have seen that Gaudreau would one day trademark his nickname. No one could have seen that he would step into the NHL, skipping the American Hockey League (AHL) completely, and score 64 points as a rookie. Or that he would follow it up by finishing in the top ten in scoring with 78 points in 79 games in his second season.

"When you see him on the TV and playing and see how they're talking about him, it's hard to believe that's our son," said Guy Gaudreau. "That it's the same old John." Maybe that's part of the reason why Gaudreau is where he is today. Nothing ever came easy.

He always had to prove himself, always had to crawl while others ran, reaching for one Skittle at a time. Because of that, maybe the next kid who is that small and talented won't have to stuff pucks in his underwear.

PITTSBURGH PENGUINS
» № 30 «

POSITION	GOALIE
CATCHES	LEFT
HEIGHT	6'4"
WEIGHT	178 LB
BORN	MAY 25, 1994
BIRTHPLACE	THUNDER BAY, ON, CAN
DRAFT	2012 PIT, 3RD RD, 22ND PK (83RD OVERALL)

Matt Murray does the splits to block Detroit Red Wings' Dylan Larkin's shot in a 2018 game. AP Photo/Carlos Osorio

WHEN A TEAM WINS THE STANLEY CUP, EVERYBODY on the roster—whether it's the leading scorer or the fourth-line forward or an anonymous scout out in Anchorage, Alaska—gets to spend a day with it. What you do in that day is entirely up to you and your imagination. The only caveat is that you have to bring along a chaperone.

As one of a few "Keepers of the Cup," Howie Borrow has seen it all. Over the years, the Cup has survived a soaking under Niagara Falls and being sunk to the bottom of Mario Lemieux's swimming pool. It's been inside steam rooms, saunas and showers, and used as a food bowl for kids, dogs and once even a Kentucky Derby winner.

The first time Phil Kessel won it in 2016, he loaded it up with hot dogs and posted a picture for all the haters who had criticized his questionable eating habits. A year later, Josh Archibald had his three-week-old son baptized in it. And then there was Matt Murray, whose wildest activity involved eating popcorn out of the Cup while watching a movie.

"It was basically a prop," Borrow said of the television that was used in a photo shoot of Murray's day, which was later posted on Twitter. "We set it up like he was watching a movie and somebody said, 'How can he be watching TV if it isn't even plugged in?'" As for the rest of the day, "He really didn't do much at all," said Borrow. "It was probably the most low-key day with the Cup I've ever had."

Matt MURRAY

On a Saturday morning in early August, Murray had just finished eating an omelette at the Valhalla Inn in Thunder Bay, Ontario, when he checked the time on his phone. He was going to be late. He quickly paid the bill, hopped into his Range Rover and headed to the airport where Borrow was due to arrive at 10 a.m. from Toronto. As soon as the Cup arrived, Murray had fourteen hours with it. And though his itinerary was light on activities, he still didn't want to waste a single minute.

Matt Murray (far right) celebrates his day with the Stanley Cup with his older brother Michael (far left) and his mom, Fenny. Photo by Michael Traikos

When Murray won the championship a year earlier as a rookie goaltender for the Pittsburgh Penguins, he had let others plan his day with the Cup. His parents had practically invited all of Thunder Bay, whether it was an old teacher he didn't remember or a former coach he didn't even know he had. He visited hospitals and hockey rinks. Even the mayor got involved. It was a non-stop party for a person who doesn't party. And before he knew it, the day was over. This time around, he was in charge, which meant a little more me-time with the trophy he had barely got to know the previous year. "Maybe take a minute for myself with the Cup this time," said Murray. "Last year, I don't even think I had a single minute."

Once it arrived at the airport, Murray loaded the Cup, which is stored in a heavy-duty lockbox on wheels, into the back of his

SUV. The first stop was Fort William Gardens, the home rink of Lakehead University's hockey team, where Murray got his first taste of playing in front of a crowd. "I still remember it was one of my first times playing net," he said. "[My team] played during the intermission of a Lakehead University game. I think there were like a thousand fans."

For the first two hours of the day, Murray got the housecleaning out of the way. He invited former coaches and family friends to take pictures with the Cup inside a tiny dressing room, and then brought it onto the rink, outside of which hundreds of locals had been lining up since 6 a.m. Murray, dressed in black workout pants and a black long-sleeved shirt, hoisted the Cup above his head as a DJ blasted "We Are the Champions." And then... that was it.

Murray retreated back to his condo with the Cup and its chaperone. Together, with his girlfriend and the black Labrador he had rescued earlier that year, they spent the rest of the day simply hanging out. A photographer arrived and they headed down to the shore and posed for a picture in front of the Sleeping Giant, a natural wonder out in Lake Superior. Later on, about twenty friends were invited to his place at night, but there was no craziness. "That was it," said Borrow. "They sat around a table talking, sharing stories, got some photos with the Cup, did some drinking out of it, but nothing crazy. The curfew for the players is midnight. He let me go early."

For those who know Murray, this wasn't surprising. As one former GM said, it's amazing he even celebrated. "You know when you win the Stanley Cup and everyone goes crazy? Well, I wasn't really sure what he'd be like, because he's such a low-key guy," said Dave Torrie, who drafted Murray to the OHL as general manager of the Sault Ste. Marie Greyhounds. "That's part of his success."

At only twenty-three years old Murray already had his name on the Stanley Cup twice, having won his first championship as a rookie and his second straight title while technically still a rookie because he had only played thirteen games in his first season. How did he do it? How did a goalie come into the league and enjoy so much early success? Well, as anyone who was on the invite list to his day with the Cup can attest, he did it by being boring.

I remember it like I was still there. We were in Superior, Wisconsin, and we were on the international ice. The extra ten yards just killed our kids. Just killed them. We were winning but the game was going the other team's way and in the last three seconds Matt let a goal in. It bounced in off a defenceman's shin pads. Bad luck. So we're in overtime. And we went six overtime periods. It was draining. It got to the point where everyone was saying just let the puck in and let's go home. But Matt, who was eleven, was not going to let up. It just gives you an indication of how he looks at the game of hockey. He was not going to lose. He was determined that he was not going to lose.

— **RICK EVOY, Murray's first goalie coach**

THERE IS A SLEEPING GIANT in Thunder Bay, Ontario. Well, two of them actually. The first is located in Lake Superior and is a giant peninsula of land composed of mountains of rock and covered in mossy grass. According to Ojibwa legend, it wasn't always rock. Many years ago a great spirit named Nanabijou was turned to stone as punishment for sharing the secret entrance to a rich silver mine that became exploited. Today, it's one of Canada's natural wonders.

You can travel to Sleeping Giant Provincial Park and hike on its many trails and even camp out on it. But the best place to view it is from way up at the top of Hillcrest Park in Thunder Bay, where you can see the entire city and where out in the distance the Sleeping Giant's dramatic steep cliffs actually resemble a man lying on his back in the water. From this vantage point, everything comes into focus. Everything seems so small, so peaceful. Violent waves crash all around the Sleeping Giant, but the great spirit doesn't wake or even budge. He just quietly endures. For a goalie, there's a lot to learn from that.

"It's a good place to sit and think," said Murray. "It's got my favourite views that I've ever seen. It's super quiet up there. Not many people." Murray took the Stanley Cup there for a picture the first time he won it in 2016. It was, as some joked, one sleeping giant celebrating with another.

Like the giant in the water, Murray was built to endure. He doesn't rattle easily. An example of that occurred in the 2016 Conference Finals, when Murray was pulled in Game 4 against the Tampa Bay Lightning, but returned to the net for Game 6 and won back-to-back starts and helped the Penguins advance to the final. Of course, there are many more examples throughout his career, whether he was playing in the NHL, the minors or as an eleven-year-old in Thunder Bay.

The story that friends and family like to tell is about the time when Murray gave up that tying goal on a fluke shot in the dying seconds of the third period and went on to play six overtime periods of perfect hockey. "It was a 6–5 game and I said, 'Oh, Matt, how are you feeling?'" said Murray's mother, Fenny. "And he was like, 'We won, didn't we?' That's all that matters to him. He's got his dad's calmness going through the world, but he's got my drive, which says I didn't sign up to lose."

From age eight, Murray knew he wanted to be a goalie. There was something about how cool the equipment looked. But at that young of an age, he had to wait. Thunder Bay wouldn't allow full-time goalies until they were older, so every team rotated their players in net based on whoever wanted to volunteer. Murray was a quiet kid. He waited until the final game of the season before putting his hand up. Once he did, it never went down.

Murray was a natural in net. He had always been a gifted athlete—he won Athlete of the Year for his entire elementary school when he was in grade three and played varsity basketball in high school—but his unusually long limbs seemed like an even better fit for grabbing pucks. "A beanpole," said Evoy. "Straight up and down."

When you are tall and skinny, you can sometimes appear awkward and gawky. Murray moved with the fluidity of a swimmer. Nothing was rushed. There was grace in his movements. "I saw a kid that was smooth," said Evoy, who coached Murray from the age of eleven to fifteen. "He wasn't one of those big, flashy, channel-nine saves-of-the-week goalies. He was just steady. I used to say, 'He's the most boring goalie you'll ever watch,' because he's never out of position."

That boring style was born out of an analytical mind that broke things down into formulas and patterns. Murray's father, who died of a heart attack in January 2018, was a lawyer and used to always say, "There's an answer to every problem." In Murray's mind, there must be a save for every shot. He was obsessive about it. As a kid, he used to watch pool trick-shot videos. But it wouldn't be enough to just watch them. Murray had to do them too. So he would practise the shots he'd seen on TV for hours until he could bounce balls over obstacles and bank them into paper bags. It was like that with everything.

Matt Murray makes a save playing road hockey in Thunder Bay. Photo courtesy of the Murray family

"A friend of mine said to me once that watching him play in net is like watching me play guitar," said Murray's older brother,

Michael. "I know what he means by that. The calmness and the technical approach and that sort of thing. Matt studies. If you talk to him about the game, he's like, *This is like this* and *This is like this*. He knows what the plays are and who's supposed to do what."

The similarities pretty well end there. Michael is the musician of the family, a talented jazz guitarist who teaches and plays in a band. "You're not going to find two more different people or life-styles as siblings," said Michael, who lives in Toronto and plays in the Ten Meter Band. "We went to the same high school but we're two years apart and ran with two of the most different crowds you could possibly imagine."

Michael was the one who moved to Toronto as soon as he could because Thunder Bay was too small. Matt did the opposite. He prefers the calm of Thunder Bay, a no-frills city of 120,000 that feels even smaller and more rural. The joke here is that the deer look both ways before crossing the road. "It's a tight-knit community," said Matt. "Once you get outside the city limits, it's probably hours before you run into another town. You're secluded."

As a kid, Matt was known for his competitive streak. He was the brother who knocked over the game of Risk if his territories were being conquered or threw the video game controller if he was losing. He was also the brother who couldn't get enough of the activity he was doing. "He was a passionate learner," said his mother. "I remember playing catch with him on the front lawn and catch wasn't good enough for him. It was always, 'Mom, throw it over there so I can dive for it.' He just aced every sport that he touched as a kid."

Matt and Michael's parents provided both children with opportunities to play sports or be involved in music. But there was one condition: you had to take it seriously. If you wanted to have fun, play road hockey or fool around on a guitar. But if you expected your parents to devote time and money into whatever you were doing, it came with responsibility—on both ends.

"We played in the Winnipeg loop," said Murray's father, Jim, "which meant we would have to get on a bus early Friday morning, play one team up there on Friday night, another team on Saturday and a third fresh team on Sunday, then get on the bus and come home. That was pretty tough, going there. One thing that Thunder Bay kids have is they learn to travel. It's a source of discipline."

"If you wanted for it to be a dream, go play fun hockey in the non-competitive level," said Murray's mom. "If you wanted it to be a goal, then we're going to work. It could be intense, but that's how it was going to be. When we went on a hockey trip, it was for Matt's hockey. We never went shopping. If I want to go on a shopping trip, I'll go with my friends. I didn't conflict the hockey trip with something else, because that's wasting other people's time."

Matt Murray plays for the Westfort Rangers in Thunder Bay. Photo courtesy of the Murray family

That line of thinking eventually led **Murray** to leave Thunder Bay. By then, he had outgrown the town and its coaches. Evoy had taught him what he knew about standard positioning and staying calm and collected in the net. But for Murray to reach the next level, he needed to do more than just be calm. The sleeping giant needed to be woken up. That's where Jon Elkin came in.

"I always said I found the diamond and Jon put the smoothness on it," said Evoy. "If there was a work ethic produced, it was from him." Murray was ten years old when he first met Elkin at a goalie camp in Toronto. The two immediately hit it off, and the Sault Ste. Marie Greyhounds later hired Elkin as the team's goalie coach for Murray's final season in the OHL. In Elkin, who is now the goalie coach of the Arizona Coyotes, Murray found a pro-style coach who "broke down the position into about one hundred drills," said Jim Murray , who passed away in January 2018. The younger Murray soaked it all up. This was exactly what he had been looking for. There was no more guesswork as to how to stop the puck. Instead, Elkin provided technical answers as to where to be and how to get there in order to make the save.

In Murray, Elkin found a goalie who had the motor skills and body control to implement everything you showed him. "Goalies can move side to side, can get into the butterfly, and utilize the same technique, but some guys have a certain fluidity, poise, that's special," said Elkin. "Carey Price is an example that everyone puts forth, and Matty also has it. Just a natural, almost effortless way of moving around the crease that's not easy to duplicate."

The next year, Murray returned for another March break session with Elkin. He added a week in the summer. Then two weeks in the summer. Eventually, Murray was spending the entire summer with Elkin, as a camp attendee while also acting as a counsellor. The two continued to work together in the summer into Murray's NHL career. "Jon Elkin's camp is very tough, it's very businesslike and not a lot of fun," said Jim Murray. "You get your money's worth. I knew Matt was serious when he said to me, 'Dad, I think I need at least two weeks with Jon Elkin this year.' That desire had come. He just grew from there to be a kind of aggressive goalie. That was the final piece."

Indeed, technique only takes you so far. After three seasons in the OHL, Murray was putting up respectable, but not exceptional, numbers. There was something missing. For all his calmness in the net and his analytical approach to the position, Murray lacked that killer instinct. "From day to day, he's not overly emotional," said Elkin. "He's competitive, but not overly emotional. He's just very even keel, off the ice and on the ice."

That's not necessarily a negative. A big reason why Murray is able to shake off a fluke goal or a bad start is because he is the sleeping giant, a goalie who does not feel the crashing of waves when he is not at his best. But if he was going to take the next step and become the type of goalie who won back-to-back Stanley Cups as a rookie—effectively pushing Marc-Andre Fleury to the backup position—he needed to tap into what he did when playing board games as a kid and allow himself to smash a stick every now and then.

"He was a big factor for me coming out of my shell," Murray said of Elkin. "The one thing that I remember him saying the most was really simple: 'At the end of the day, the best goalies in the world are the ones that compete and read the play.' And those are the two things that have stuck with me to this day. I still remember the day when he told me that. It was the year before my draft year. It was a big year for me. He was a huge factor for me, definitely, to come out of my shell a little bit and show that passion."

One summer David Clarkson, an NHL forward and Toronto native, came to Elkin's camp to take shots on the goalies. During one drill, Clarkson cut hard toward the net and Murray backed off and gave up his crease to the older and more physical player. Elkin went over to Murray: "You're going to let him do that to you? Get angry! This is your crease!" Elkin then went over to Clarkson: "Do that again," he said. "Go even harder." This time, Murray held his ground and knocked Clarkson down.

"In goaltending, it's not always two plus two equals four," said Elkin. "There's a lot of variables that don't add up and you have to scramble and make it up as you go along and learn to read and react. That part started to click for him as a nineteen-year-old. That was the last essential ingredient he needed."

DUBAS, WHO WAS BORN IN Sault Ste. Marie, was hired as assistant general manager of the Toronto Maple Leafs when he was only twenty-eight years old, to help kick-start the team's rebuild. Four years earlier, he had become the youngest general manager in the history of the OHL. Ask him which job put more wrinkle lines on his face and there's no questioning the answer.

> I don't know if you've ever been to the Soo, but it's a great place to work and play if you're going to go into a high-pressure spot, because it's the only show in town. It's sold out every game and every day in the newspaper there's three or four articles about the team. It's non-stop.
>
> — **KYLE DUBAS, former GM of the Sault Ste. Marie Greyhounds**

The OHL's 2011–12 season had not even started when Dubas got into a public spat with the sports editor of the local paper after he was accused of "stringing along" an over-age goalie who was then placed on waivers. Two months later, Dubas made national news—and earned a reputation as a brash and bold general manager who was not afraid to swing for the fences—by packaging six draft picks and two players in a blockbuster trade for Jack Campbell, who a year earlier was the No. 11 pick in the NHL Entry Draft. "I knew it was complicated and I knew the risks of the trade full well," said Dubas. "It did not pay off for us."

Why did he make the trade? Two reasons: Campbell, who was the best goalie in junior hockey, was available, and Dubas's other goalie, Murray, was unproven. Human beings sometimes falter under pressure—especially young ones lacking experience. That was what Dubas was thinking at the time of the trade. But he wasn't necessarily thinking it about himself. That year, the Greyhounds had jumped out to a 10–6–0 record and pushed their way into third place. It was somewhat unexpected for a team that had finished with the third-worst record the previous year. And

Dubas, who was an early proponent of advanced stats, was skeptical it could last.

"I wasn't really expecting us to be a contending team," said Dubas. "Everything underlying was pointing to the fact that we weren't really as good as our record had indicated. We were ranked in the top ten in Canada at one point in November. But we were basically getting outshot every night."

Most of the early success that season was due to Murray, the goalie who had pushed over-ager Chris Perugini to the curb and was now trying to position himself as a top NHL draft pick. But Dubas had his doubts. For one, Murray had played just twenty-eight games the year before. Judging by his frail body ("He was the same height as he is now, but even skinnier," said Dubas. "I don't even know if he was 165 pounds. I doubt it.") and the number of shots he was facing on a nightly basis, it was only a matter of time before he caved.

"So we got off to a good start and we were getting badly outshot and the owner said to me, 'Can we keep going?' I said the only way we can keep going is if we improve a lot of facets in our team. But basically, we were going to need to get all-world goaltending throughout. And the expectations on Matt would have been too great. Jack came available and our owners were antsy to keep everything rolling. We had missed the playoffs two of the previous three years. With me being a younger manager, we went for it." Making the trade was the easy part. Breaking the news to Murray took some finessing.

Depending on traffic and how efficiently the drive-through at McDonald's could handle twenty-five or so orders of burgers and fries, the bus ride from Sault Ste. Marie to Peterborough usually took about eight hours. It was during a road trip on November 2 that Dubas called Murray to the front of the bus and told him he was essentially now the team's backup goalie.

That's not how Dubas actually broke the news, but that's all Murray heard.

"I just explained to Matt why we did what we did, that 'You are probably going to take this as an indictment about you, but it's not,'" said Dubas. "He was like anybody would be in that case. He was very quiet."

"To be honest, I was pissed off," said Murray. "I was extremely pissed off. But at the end of the day, you're part of a team and you're part of something bigger, so I wasn't going to let any hard feelings linger or anything like that. I knew exactly who Jack Campbell was and he was kind of everything I wanted to be at the time. He was a first-round pick and he had already signed an NHL contract. He was one of the best goalie prospects in the world. I was pissed off. But as a kid, I was fairly quiet and didn't want to step on anyone else's toes, so I definitely held my emotions."

Jack Campbell was an all-world goalie, someone who had led the US to a World Junior Championship title and in 2011 was considered a top NHL prospect. But Murray also knew that the Greyhounds were winning games and were on track to make the playoffs and it was largely because of him. And now, he was being pushed to the curb for an even better goalie. It wasn't really fair. Worst of all, Murray was in his draft year. Every team in the NHL was scouting him and would now be wondering why the Greyhounds needed to acquire Campbell in the trade. Would they think Murray wasn't good enough to be a starter? That he wasn't a good teammate?

All these thoughts ran through Murray's head. But he tried not to let it show. He just sat there, unable to sleep, thinking about what he was going to say to his newest teammate. When the bus finally reached Peterborough the next morning, Campbell was waiting outside. Unprompted, Murray beat his teammates to the front of the bus and was the first to get off. He walked up to

Campbell and extended a hand to the player who had come to take his job. "Welcome to the team," said Murray.

"I remember it like it was yesterday," said Campbell. "I just remember how cool of a feeling that was. I knew that he was a highly touted kid and I was taking some of his ice time, and to show the character he had to welcome me to the team, that was really impressive and made me feel good."

"He's waiting for us and you're thinking how is everyone going to respond to this?" said Dubas. "The team had missed the play-offs the year before and none of these guys have had any success and you're bringing in this decorated goalie. Everyone knows who Jack Campbell is. They're kind of excited, but at the same time they're real tight with Matt. It's one of those uneasy things. And to Matt's credit, he breaks the ice by immediately walking up to him and welcoming him to the team. But that's Matt. Normally, it's a nineteen- or a twenty-year-old doing that. It's usually not the seventeen-year-old goalie."

About a week later, Murray invited Campbell over to his billet's house. The place had a huge backyard with a barn and plenty of forested area perfect for playing paintball. Campbell had never played. Murray had his own gun. "The competitive side came out and he shot me right between the eyes in my face mask," said Campbell. "I just remember I was like, 'I really like this guy a lot.' He's like me at heart with how competitive he is. But I learned pretty quickly not to go over to Matt's and play paintball."

Despite Murray and Campbell hitting it off—"Jack happens to be one of the best people you'll ever meet," said Murray—the tandem turned out to be a two-headed monster. Part of it was out of their control. All those underlying numbers that Dubas was worried about bubbled to the surface. The Greyhounds lost ten of their next eleven games, were never really able to rebound and finished out of the playoffs. "Mentally, I was a little bit out of it," said Campbell. "I could've played a lot better to help the team to win. And Matt was really young, obviously."

"Any of our team's lack of success that year was not because of our goaltending," said Dubas. "If you look at the talent of the team, we were not set up to contend." Worse yet, Murray was not set up for the 2012 draft. In January of that year, NHL Central Scouting had ranked him as the second-highest goaltender in North America. But that was before he finished the season with a 4.08 goals-against average and .876 save percentage, a downgrade from the year before.

"The big trade was definitely a setback," said Murray's dad. "And that's the difference with his coach right now. [Mike Sullivan] says 'I think you can do it. I don't care about your age or experience or whatever.' Where, when he was playing in the Soo, they traded for a more experienced goalie down there, even though Matt was winning and playing well at the time. That did set him back."

Murray's stats didn't tell the entire story. But because he played in only half the games that year, stats were all scouts had to go by. NHL teams who should have been clamouring for a wiry yet athletic 6-foot-4 goalie with a huge wingspan were now unsure of his potential simply because they didn't get to see him enough. When they did, he was getting pummelled. In the 2012 NHL Entry Draft, Murray was selected in the third round, eighty-third overall, behind nine other goalies.

"That draft year, I was working as a scout with the Buffalo Sabres and I was a little surprised he wasn't more highly rated as a goaltender compared to other goalies in the same birth year," said Torrie. "But he got stuck in a backup role as a seventeen-year-old so teams had a hard time seeing him play. I thought he played good at the U-18s that spring. It just seemed that there wasn't a lot of traction. We brought him into Buffalo at the time, but the decision-makers didn't really feel comfortable—they didn't feel they got enough views of him. They had my opinion on him, but they hadn't seen him enough. I'm sure there were a lot of teams thinking that way."

After the draft, Murray returned to Sault Ste. Marie. Campbell was now gone and Murray finally had the net to himself. Well, sort of. The team got off to another hot start, with Murray posting even better numbers, but then he went into a rut and temporarily lost the job to Justin Nichols. By the time the playoffs arrived, Dubas was being stopped on the street by fans wondering who was going to start: Murray or Nichols.

The team went with Murray, who played well against Owen Sound, but the team lost in the first round. Some fans blamed Murray. So when the Greyhounds traded Nichols at the start of the following season, it wasn't met with overwhelming support from the fan base. "The day that we traded Justin Nichols was two or three days before the season and we always introduce our players to the season-ticket holders and then I have to do this town hall where they ask me questions," said Dubas. "And I remember that year, one of the most prominent fans who never missed a thing, said 'I see you're missing a goalie.' The trade had not been approved yet, but there were rumours, so he said, 'If you've moved Justin Nichols, then I'm curious why you've moved the wrong goalie.'"

Murray was on the stage. Dubas did his best to fan out the flames and answer the question without losing his temper. He then looked over at Murray. The goalie smiled at him and stood quietly. The sleeping giant doesn't get bothered by waves.

"His ability to deal with crap and to push through and come out on the other side better is outstanding," said Dubas. "It's like, the team wasn't very good and then the next year we go out and make a trade for a goalie, make a coaching change, the fans want the flavour of the day, and then as a nineteen-year-old that year he was outstanding. He should have been on the World Junior team."

MURRAY'S RECORD-BREAKING shutout streak in the AHL lasted an entire month. But talk to his former minor-league teammates and they'll tell you that was nothing. Murray used to go even longer without allowing a goal in practice. And he faced three times as many shots. "When he was a rookie, we used to play this game of four-on-four at the end of a practice and most goalies hate it, because they just get shot at all the time and they give up lots of goals," said Tom Kostopoulos, who was the captain of the Wilkes-Barre/Scranton Penguins. "But he didn't complain. He just battled for every puck. He played every puck to the death, like it was the last puck in Game 7 of the Stanley Cup final."

"I don't want to say I'm surprised, because I knew he could do it. But to do it that quickly was really impressive. It was almost one of those things where you're surprised but not surprised. When he was in a zone and it was looking like he was going to win every game he started, we were like, 'Ok, we might have to make a decision late in the year.'"

— JOHN HYNES, former head coach, Wilkes-Barre/ Scranton Penguins

When Murray arrived at Wilkes-Barre/Scranton in 2014, the expectation was that he was going to have to battle for ice time. Marc-Andre Fleury was already entrenched as the Pittsburgh Penguins' No. 1 goalie and the team had just signed Thomas Greiss to be Fleury's backup, pushing Jeff Zatkoff back down to the AHL. The question was whether Murray, who was twenty years old, would benefit from playing behind Zatkoff in the AHL or whether it was better for his development to get starting goalie minutes in the East Coast Hockey League (ECHL).

Murray answered that question early on. No one could see that this was someone who in another year would be hoisting the first of two Stanley Cups in the NHL, but there were signs that Murray was ahead of the curve. He wasn't a typical AHL rookie. He had a level of professionalism and maturity that belied his age.

He practised hard, played even harder and didn't take any nights off. His teammates respected him almost instantly.

That last part should not be overlooked. The goaltending position takes a long time to master at the top level. Most goalies don't become NHL starters when they are twenty-one years old. Even fewer win championships as a rookie. It takes time to master the finer arts of the position. How did Murray get so good so fast? According to his teammates in Pittsburgh and in Wilkes-Barre/Scranton, he earned their respect.

The best example of this is the four-on-four mini-games that concluded every practice. Minor-league practices are longer than NHL practices, because AHL teams load up their games on weekends, allowing coaches to spend twice as long on the ice during the week. By the end of a practice, players are exhausted. At the same time, the best time to work on individual skills is when the coaches are off the ice and you can fool around and try different breakaway moves or one-timers from positions that you might not dare in a game-like setting.

The problem is that you need a goalie to shoot on. And whereas the veteran—or starting goalie—usually is allowed to hit the showers early, the backup typically has to stay and play the role of the "shooter tutor."

"In those kinds of games, you're not really defending too hard," said forward Conor Sheary. "You're working on your skills and there's a lot of breakaways and two-on-ones. And here's Murray, making all these huge saves. It was fun to watch, but annoying as a player because you're like, 'Hey, let me score.'" It was annoying to have a goalie rob you of your confidence in practice. But the flip side of that, said Wilkes-Barre/Scranton captain Tom Kostopoulos, is that you wanted to battle for the goalie who was willing to battle every puck to the death to make you better.

"I was just amazed by how competitive he was," said Kostopoulos. "Any time he got scored on in practice, he'd get so upset. I liked to always shoot on him, because you knew if you ever got one by him, it was a good shot. It made you better."

When Zatkoff got hurt, Murray made a seamless transition into the top spot. That's when the shutout streak started. From February 8 to March 8—exactly 304 minutes and 11 seconds— Murray stopped every shot he faced and recorded four consecutive shutouts. For nearly six games, he was perfect. Breakaways, two-on-ones, deflections, rebounds, one-timers from the slot and knucklers from the point—Murray saved them all. It was magical. And yet, like any good illusionist, the best part about the trick was that he made it look so easy.

"He would make all the easy saves and make the hard saves look easy and a couple of times a game he would make an incredible save where he reached back and threw his pad across," said Kostopoulos. "If you didn't practice with him, you'd say, 'My God, how did he do that?' But for us guys who practiced with him, he was doing that ten times a day in practice. We'd seen it before."

Murray treated the streak similarly. He broke an AHL record, a heck of an achievement for a rookie. When the streak finally ended, Murray didn't take a moment to celebrate what he had done. With 1:11 remaining in the third period of a 4–1 win against the Springfield Falcons, he simply focused on stopping the next shot.

"It was funny, because the incredible thing about it was his demeanour never changed," said John Hynes, who was then the head coach of the team. "He was like the same guy every day. It was like it was an exhibition game for him. That's when we were all like, 'We might have something special here.' It was almost like he was a ten-year veteran, a true professional. Even now, I watch him in the playoffs and he's the same."

When the season ended, Murray led all goalies in the AHL with a 1.58 goals-against average, a .941 save percentage and 12 shutouts—five more than the goalie with the next highest total.

Not surprisingly, he was named the league's top goalie and top rookie. The Pittsburgh Penguins tabbed him as the goalie of the future. The only question was how far in the future that would be.

MURRAY BEGAN THE FOLLOWING SEASON IN THE AHL, because the Penguins still had Fleury as their No. 1 goalie and Murray was better off playing games in the minors than sitting on the bench as an NHL backup. "The plan was not to keep him in the AHL all year," said Penguins GM Jim Rutherford. "The plan was to bring him up at the deadline."

That being said, the plan was still for Murray to back up Fleury—not take his job. But plans change. By the time the play-offs began, Fleury, who had been out with a concussion, was now back but no doubt rusty. Murray took advantage of the opportunity. Despite playing in only thirteen regular season games, Murray outplayed the New York Rangers' Henrik Lundqvist and the Washington Capitals' Braden Holtby, and led the Penguins to their first Stanley Cup championship in seven years. "We felt pretty strongly that he was ready to go at that time," said Rutherford. "As it turns out, he definitely was."

A year later, Murray was injured at the start of the playoffs but returned to the net for Game 4 of the Conference Finals and once again led the Penguins to the Finals, where they won back-to-back championships. And he celebrated too. But he did it in typical Murray fashion: understated and without much fanfare.

Aaron EKBLAD

FLORIDA PANTHERS
» № 5 «

POSITION	DEFENCE
SHOOTS	RIGHT
HEIGHT	6'4"
WEIGHT	216 LB
BORN	FEBRUARY 7, 1996
BIRTHPLACE	WINDSOR, ON, CAN
DRAFT	2014 FLA, 1ST RD, 1ST PK (1ST OVERALL)

Aaron Ekblad and Vancouver Canucks' Thomas Vanek fight over the puck during a 2018 game. AP Photo/Wilfredo Lee

EXCEPTIONAL. AT ONE TIME, BEFORE EVERY TOP-three draft pick was deemed a "generational talent," the word *exceptional* still meant something. To be exceptional was to be truly special, different from the rest, extraordinary. The great Bobby Orr was exceptional. So were Wayne Gretzky, Mario Lemieux and Sidney Crosby. In 2005, after John Tavares had scored 91 goals and 158 points in 72 games in minor midget, he became the first player granted "exceptional status" so that he could join the Oshawa Generals at fifteen years old. By definition, he was literally the first exception to the rule.

Six years later came another exception. But first, Ekblad had to answer an essay question: "What Attributes Do You Possess that Will Make You Capable of Playing in the OHL?" In other words, what made him exceptional? Ekblad wrote the entire essay on his phone. Seriously, he did. He would type out a paragraph while in class at school and then come home and edit it for spelling and grammar at night. It took him forever—it's not easy typing with only your thumbs, especially with the autocorrect function turned on. "You have to write essays, have psych evaluations and have all that kind of stuff," said Ekblad. "The hoops are crazy, there's no doubt about it."

Looking back, he probably could have written the thing in crayon and been accepted. That's how easy a decision it was. "There were never any doubts, never any questioning. Never," said CHL president David Branch, who developed the criteria to determine whether a player is granted exceptional status. "He was just so mature, not just on the ice but off it as well."

At the time he applied, Ekblad was a 6-foot-2 and 205-pound "man-child," as one coach called him. He was already playing a year above his age group with the Sun County Panthers, with whom he had won a league championship, and was named to the All-Ontario All-Star Team. He wasn't just the biggest and best player in his age group, he was the biggest and best among kids who had a year on him. Getting exceptional status seemed nothing more than a formality. After all, Bauer had already sent him sticks with his name engraved on them and teammates were already calling him "First Ovie," in reference to his destiny to be the first overall pick in the OHL Priority Draft—as well as the NHL Entry Draft that was still years away. "It's hard to say in four years that kid's going to be the first overall pick in the NHL," said Barrie Colts general manager Jason Ford. "But with Aaron, you just knew that he had all those qualities."

Typing during the day and editing at night, Ekblad listed the many reasons why he could handle the OHL a year early, everything from his imposing size and skating ability to how he could fend off an attacking forechecker when going back in the defensive zone for a puck ("It's about angling, proper angling and my game is getting the puck and turning it from south to north as quickly as possible"). On and on he went, talking about his maturity and leadership skills, his grades and hockey IQ, his family support, his slapshot, his two-way game...

He could have listed even more. He could have said he was so strong that once, when playing barefoot hockey in the basement, he accidentally broke his older brother's foot—"Toe," said Ekblad, interrupting. "It was just his big toe"—with a particularly hard pass. He could have mentioned that it wasn't just hockey that he excelled at, that "he was known as the eighth-grader who could dunk," according to childhood friend Brandon Lalonde.

He could have said that he was already shaving, but never swore, that he was always the first to a post-whistle scrum but the last one to fight. If he'd wanted to save some time typing, he could have simply snapped a photo of his class picture, the one where Ekblad is two feet taller than some of the other kids—"It was kind of comical at times," said his mother, Lisa—or offered the phone number of his hockey agent, Bobby Orr, who many years earlier played in the OHL as a fourteen-year-old and told Ekblad that he could handle it.

"The tipping point was Bobby Orr was an advocate for it," Ekblad said. "At first, he was like 'maybe you shouldn't do it, [but] because you're a big fish playing in a small pond with kids your own age, I think that will be good for you.' [My family's] question to him was, 'You did it—do you have any regrets?' And he was like, 'No, not at all.' So we kind of ran with that. If he could do it—and obviously I'm not comparing myself to Bobby Orr, he's the best defenceman that ever played—but if he could do it, and it was good for him, then maybe it could be good for me. And it was."

Ekblad, who was the first defenceman granted exceptional status, was the first overall pick of the Florida Panthers in 2014. In his first season in the NHL, he won the Calder Memorial Trophy as the league's top rookie, having scored 12 goals and 39 points in 81 games while averaging nearly 22 minutes a game as an eighteen-year-old. It wasn't particularly flashy. Others scored more goals, produced more points and found their way onto more highlight reels. But Ekblad, whose most exceptional quality was his maturity, was exceptionally consistent.

"If you look back at guys who are high-end NHL defencemen, it takes a few years," said Bob Boughner, Ekblad's head coach in Florida and a friend of the family. "The uniqueness of Aaron is with his strength and his skating and how big he is; I think he can play a hard-nosed defensive game down low. But I also think he can run a power play up top. He's a new-aged two-way defenceman. I had the pleasure of coaching Brent Burns for the last couple of years in San Jose and he's got an unreal shot and he's unreal offensively, but I don't think Brent gets enough credit for how good he is defensively. I see a little of that in Aaron. Obviously, he's a lot younger and lot more inexperienced, but he can be that fourth forward that jumps up and is that offensive guy and also plays against top offensive guys."

THEY NEEDED A GOAL. THERE WERE ONLY ABOUT THIRTEEN SECONDS LEFT in the game and the Sun County Panthers were trailing by one. The coach called a time out and pulled the players toward the bench so that they could plan their attack. "Ekblad," said head coach Todd Lalonde. "I want you to play wing."

Ekblad, who had been a defenceman his entire life, was hesitant. "What do I do?" he asked.

"Listen," said the coach, "you're a big guy, and I need to move you to the front of the net because you've got great touch." Lalonde then got out a black marker and started scribbling furiously on a small whiteboard, drawing arrows that pointed toward the net. He looked at Ekblad, who seemed even more confused. "Where do you want me to line up?"

"All I want you to do is score," said Lalonde. A few moments later, the players lined up for the offensive-zone faceoff. Ekblad, who was the biggest kid on the ice even though he was also a year younger than everyone, lined up on the wing and took a look at his surroundings. "Just score," he said to himself. Okay, he could do that.

"So they won the faceoff and immediately he runs the defenceman over," said Lalonde, remembering the play like it was yesterday. "Then he grabs the puck and takes about two steps to the middle of the ice and puts it under the bar. At the end of the day, we needed a goal and he just did it."

GETTING INTO THE OHL A YEAR EARLY TURNED OUT TO BE easy. It was playing above his age group in the Sun County Minor Hockey Association that was the bigger challenge. Ekblad was ten years old when his father asked if he could play on a team with the eleven-year-olds. It was a reasonable request. Ekblad was nearly six feet tall by then, easily the biggest kid in his age group. Some kids hit growth spurts early on and can seem gawky, like they are all arms and legs. Ekblad wasn't clumsy. He was confident in his body, a naturally smooth skater who handled the puck with ease. "Well, he certainly had a size advantage," said Lisa Ekblad. "He was a big kid. And he was fortunate enough to be fairly coordinated."

"I can remember vividly that first workout," said coach Lalonde. "We did a breakout drill and this kid takes three strides to go and pursue a puck in the defensive zone and I'm like, 'Wow.' His first three steps were something else."

By ten years old, Ekblad was already becoming something of a known commodity. Part of it was that he was just so big and so talented. The other part was that he was a big fish in a really small pond, having grown up in Belle River, Ontario, which sits on Lake St. Clair on the Canadian side of the US border, about a half-hour's drive from Windsor. With its population of less than forty thousand, everyone is connected in one way or another. For instance, Dave and Lisa Ekblad were high school sweethearts who were introduced by Windsor Spitfires head coach Warren Rychel, who once coached Aaron at a pro skate with Bob Boughner, who also grew up with Dave and Lisa and later became Aaron's NHL head coach with the Florida Panthers.

"It's a small-town feel," said Ekblad, who bought a house not far from where he grew up. "My mom's a nurse practitioner and obviously she's bound by confidentiality, but a lot of people in the community would be like, 'Your mom's my nurse practitioner,' or 'I know your dad real well, I play Monday night hockey with him.' I have a lot of fun with that."

Ekblad gets his size and athleticism from his dad, a former goalie who is about the same size as his son, "minus a few extra pounds," Dave Ekblad joked. His mom said she wasn't much of an athlete ("Nothing that I would ever want to admit to"), but it's clear that Aaron got his mom's humility and thoughtfulness. He was always embarrassed by extra attention growing up, once asking an equipment manufacturer to stop sending him sticks with his name engraved on them because he didn't want to seem above the team.

As for the maturity, both parents throw up their hands. That's all Aaron, they say. He has a quiet confidence about him, as though this is his second go-around in life. As a result, he was also the first person friends would turn to when there was a problem. "My first year of school away at university, we talked for two hours," said Brandon Lalonde. "He was getting ready for the NHL draft and I was a little homesick and he spent two hours talking to me on the phone. He's that kind of guy."

Sports played a huge role in Ekblad's upbringing. His older brother Darien was named after Red Wings' defenceman Darien Hatcher—Joe Louis Arena in Detroit is thirty-four kilometres away from Belle River—and their father used to jokingly tell the two boys they could be two things in life: a lefty pitcher or a righty defenceman, since both were always in high demand.

Whereas Aaron became the righty defenceman, his older brother opted to be a goalie like their dad. It was a perfect relationship. Darien needed someone to take shots on him and Aaron needed someone to practise his shots on. Sometimes, the practice ended up in the emergency room. "They weren't too bright," said Dave Ekblad, referring to the time when Aaron broke his brother's toe.

As a kid, Ekblad used to wear No. 19 in honour of Steve Yzerman, before switching to Nicklas Lidström's No. 5. Not that he even needed a number to identify him. "Everywhere we went, he was the talk of the city," said Todd Murphy, a former teammate in

Sun County. "He had a big reputation. He was a big kid who could move and shoot the puck and he was just so smart. He was already developed past kids who were probably two years older than him."

No question, playing in small-town Ontario added to the mystique. "Playing in Belle River, I remember the most kids we ever had at tryouts was forty kids, maybe," said Ekblad. "You go to try out and if you're good enough you make it. I felt a lot of the politics were put to the wayside, because it was a smaller organization." The lack of nepotism, however, cut both ways. Although Ekblad was clearly big enough and good enough to play up a year ("He always had two feet on some kids—that's a fact," said childhood friend Patrick Murphy), the Sun County Minor Hockey Association had rules. And unlike the OHL, the league was not going to make an exception— no matter how exceptional the player was.

"Ironically, he followed [NHL first-round picks] Matt Puempel and Kerby Rychel through our organization and we were just in a process of dealing with that common issue of parents who want their kids to play up right

Aaron Ekblad's 2007–2008 hockey card foreshadowed what was to come for the young defenceman—he was to become a star. Photo courtesy of the Ekblad family

from the beginning," said Richard Ofner, the former president of Sun County Minor Hockey Association, who is now retired. "There's parents who want to move their kids up every year. And it just becomes a big debate. The Ontario Minor Hockey Association

(OMHA) developed a policy where you have to rate each player and to move up they have to be either a top forward or a top defenceman. And that's such a difficult thing to do. It's much easier to flat-out say no. And Aaron was one of those players who was told no."

For three years, Dave Ekblad tried to get his son to play up. For three years, the answer was the same. He would have to wait until he was thirteen before he was allowed to move up. Other parents might have raised a stink or moved their kid to another hockey association, where the rules were less rigid. But the Ekblads accepted the decision, trusting that the hockey association had its reasons and was operating with their son's best interests in mind.

It was a life lesson for Ekblad. No matter how hard you might try, some things are out of your control. It's how you respond to adversity that defines the person you are. "Could he have played up? Yeah, he could have. But we didn't feel it hurt his development," said Ofner. "We actually felt that dominating at a young age was a good thing. By the time he got to minor bantam it was perfect. He fit right in there and for the first month he was probably their top defenceman. It became a lot easier after that. Whenever parents came forward and said, we want our son to move up, all we had to say was, 'We turned down Aaron Ekblad and we don't think it hurt his development.'"

When he was thirteen, Ekblad was finally allowed to move up. And the timing could not have been better. While Ekblad was finally moving up, Lalonde was moving down. A former junior hockey standout as a two-way centre, Lalonde had spent six years behind the bench of the Sudbury Wolves before coaching numerous semi-pro teams in Texas. Newly divorced and looking for a change of scenery, he had moved with his son to Windsor, where he got a sales job working with Ofner's wife at a Toyota dealership. "We had a coach back out on us because he got a job with the

Leamington Flyers," said Ofner. "So at the last minute we needed a coach. Todd Lalonde was there and we asked if he was interested and he ended up taking the job."

"I really didn't know anyone in Windsor or the Sun County area," said Lalonde. "What's interesting is when I was asked to coach the minor bantam team, the convener said 'there's a caveat to this story and the caveat is that there's this kid who we're going to allow to play a year up, but we want you to tell us based on your hockey background'— and I'd coached major junior for eight or nine years in Sudbury— 'if we're doing the right or the wrong thing, because we're not convinced the minor hockey officials are reading this right.' And I said, 'Sure, but I'll be honest with you: why would you rush a kid's development?' Without even seeing him, I was conditioned to believe that the kid should just play at his age level and be a star."

Aaron Ekblad used to wear No. 19 in honour of Steve Yzerman. He switched to No. 5 in honour of Nicklas Lidström, and continues to wear No. 5 with the Florida Panthers.
Photo courtesy of the Ekblad family

Of course, his mind changed quickly after meeting the so-called kid, who turned out to be bigger and stronger and faster than Lalonde could have imagined. With just a few strides, Ekblad covered great distances. He made tape-to-tape passes. But it was more than that. Even in the first practice, Ekblad was pushing Lalonde to take it up a notch—not the other way around.

"Ek would say to me, 'When you're dumping pucks in I want you to dump them in right along the boards so it's really tough for me to get,'" said Lalonde. "And this is a kid who's twelve years old. But he's perceptive enough to know that the harder you work in practice, the easier it's going to be in a game. At that point, I knew there was something really special in this kid."

Lalonde was a perfect fit for a player who was playing up a year and would later enter the OHL as a fifteen-year-old. He coached the kids like they were pros, demanding a lot of them both on and off the ice. But he also knew how to keep the mood light, often making himself the butt of jokes when delivering a message on the importance of putting the team in front of yourself.

A favourite story of Lalonde's was when he had tried out for Canada's World Junior Championship team in 1988. He got cut. But as Lalonde tells it, it was really his fault. The coach had put him on a line with a kid who also wanted to play centre. "I can't play with this guy," Lalonde had told the coach. "I've got to play centre." So the team sent Lalonde home. The other guy, meanwhile, helped lead Canada to a gold medal and then went on to play twenty years in the NHL. "You might have heard of him," said Lalonde. "His name was Joe Sakic." "Todd is very humble," said Ofner. "Some guys would never admit a story like that."

Lalonde added structure to Ekblad's game. In the past, it wasn't unusual for coaches to double-shift Ekblad and let him stay on the ice for the entire game. Lalonde taught Ekblad to pace himself, to play hard for ninety-second bursts. He also challenged Ekblad to be perfect in his own end, telling him that there was never an excuse for having a forward deke around him. "He just said to me, 'You don't get beat—ever,'" said Ekblad. "'Two-on-ones, yeah, you're going to get beat sometimes. Three-on-ones, you're going to get beat, three-on-twos you're going to get beat, but one-on-ones you never ever get beat.' And that's something that I've held near and dear to my heart forever. It's you against one other person. There's no edge. You should be better than that person and that's kind of what I've held onto."

It wasn't just technical skills that Lalonde impressed upon the kids. He taught them how to become men. Sure, all hockey players—whether NHLers or six-year-olds playing competitively—arrive at the rink wearing a dress shirt and tie. But that was just the start for Lalonde's teams. *Respect* was a word that carried a lot of weight. There was no backtalk, no teasing, not even a curse word allowed—ever.

"He wouldn't let any of us swear in the dressing room," said Ekblad. "If he caught you swearing, he'd put you into the back of the car and send you home. He was a very disciplined guy. Kept us really disciplined and it was very fun playing for him."

"I got kicked out of practice," said Trevor Murphy. "I remember to this day. I made a bad pass and just reacted by swearing out something. He's like, 'No, you can't be doing that.' You learn. We always learned from our mistakes from him and he always corrected them the right way." It's difficult to say whether a swear jar was the reason the Sun County Panthers won the alliance championship. But there's no doubt that Lalonde's emphasis on respecting your teammates brought the team together. The players, who came from different schools and had their own circles of friends, started spending more time together while away from the rink.

"He's an amazing hockey coach," Brandon Lalonde said of his dad. "I wouldn't even say we had the horses. I think we thought we were better than we actually were and that was something that my dad worked to instill in us and something that we talk about to this day. When you compared us on paper to other teams, we shouldn't have beat them. But we bought in so hard and were so invested in what we wanted to do that no one was going to beat us. We went into every game knowing that we were going to win."

Then again, it's easy to feel that way when you've got a defence-man who is literally exceptional.

THE GUYS NEEDED TO CHECK THEIR EGOS AT THE DOOR. THAT'S HOW IT started. That's why Todd Lalonde shut the dressing room door after a brutal loss and started one of his famous lectures. It was early in the season, but the Sun County Panthers weren't playing like a team, he said. They were playing like twenty-three individuals who were more concerned about padding their stats and auditioning for the scouts in the rink than actually winning a game. "You know, guys," Lalonde said, "I know it's your midget minor year, I know all you guys are thinking about getting drafted..."

As he spoke, Lalonde started to scan the faces in the room, making sure everyone felt like he was talking directly to them. And then he looked at Ekblad, who was listening but not really paying as much attention as the others, since he was another year from the OHL Priority Draft. "Ekblad," said Lalonde. "Even Ekblad's thinking about getting drafted."

Suddenly, Ekblad sat up in his seat. "Todd, I wasn't thinking about getting drafted," he said.

"Well, why not?"

HE DIDN'T LIKE THE "FIRST OVIE" NICKNAME, BY THE WAY, the same way he didn't like getting sticks sent to him with "EKBLAD" engraved on the shaft. It was another thing that made him stand out above the team. "I was with him one day and he called the guy who was sending him the sticks and was like, 'You've got to stop putting my name on the sticks, because I hate the way people look at me and say how did you get your name on your sticks?'" Brandon Lalonde said of Ekblad. "'Just send me the regular sticks. Pretend like it's no one.'"

Of course, he wasn't just an average player. That was clear to anyone who had seen him play up that year. "Bigger than most, faster than many, but smarter than all of them," is how Lalonde described Ekblad to visiting scouts and anyone who asked if the fourteen-year-old was really as good as people were saying he was. It was Lalonde who suggested Ekblad should apply for exceptional status—and then started calling him "First Ovie" because, once accepted, Ekblad was clearly going to be chosen first overall in the OHL Priority Draft. "As a fourteen-year-old, you could have put him in the lineup for Barrie on a Thursday night in Oshawa and he could have done as good as any defenceman any team had," said Lalonde. "He was certainly gifted, but he had a want and desire to be the best."

To no one's surprise, there had been no adjustment period for Ekblad during his year of playing up with Sun County. One month into the season and Lalonde said, "He had already sort of became the Nick Lidström–type defenceman."

Aaron Ekblad played for the Sun County Panthers for many years. Photo courtesy of the Ekblad family

The comparison to Lidström was lofty and yet it was also appropriate. Like the seven-time Norris Trophy winner, Ekblad wasn't particularly flashy. He didn't rush the puck up the ice, deke through a pile of defenders and then roof the puck over the goalie's glove. Nor did he put anyone through the boards with glass-rattling bodychecks. He played textbook defence. He was more efficient than energetic, the kind of player who was always where he was supposed to be and who almost always made the right pass.

"The one thing we stressed for all those kids in their draft year was there's nothing worse than a defenceman who can't play defence," said Lalonde. "And parents at the minor hockey level get caught up in the kids' ability to jump out and contribute to the offensive side of the game, be it five-on-five or power play. And what I tried to teach these kids was when you learn to play defence positionally inside the faceoff dots, toe caps facing up the ice, moving your head not your feet, then you're in a position to play offence whenever you want or when the opportunity presents itself.

"And Ek was like a sponge. He would instinctively know where he was in all three zones. If he was going to get beat, he was going to get beat on the outside and never get beat to the goalpost. He really understood the defensive principles, which in minor hockey is sort of odd."

The first time Lalonde mentioned exceptional status to Ekblad was during that post-game lecture on playing as a team. Afterward, the two talked more about it. "That was the first time it dawned on me," said Ekblad. "I had heard of the exceptional status rule, but I didn't think I could do it. And Todd was like, 'Yeah, for sure you can. There's a 100 per cent chance you'll get in.'"

After Tavares had been granted exceptional status to join the OHL early, another forward had applied and been rejected. Ekblad was the first defenceman to apply and the OHL's concerns were different. Ekblad was bigger than Tavares had been when he entered the league as a fifteen-year-old, but they played different positions and were different players. As many skilled goal scorers did, Tavares went out of his way to avoid contact. Ekblad's job as a defenceman was to initiate contact. As strong as he was, he would be getting physical against players who were a lot more physically mature.

"When I first met him and his mom and dad, I said, 'Listen, Aaron, one of the concerns that we have is you've got to go back to your own zone and pick up that puck and you're going to have guys at the age of nineteen and twenty coming at you pretty hard. Do you think you're ready to handle that?'" said David Branch. "And right away he said, 'Oh, Mr. Branch, listen, first of all it's all about angling, proper angling, and my game is getting the puck and turning it from south to north as quickly as possible.'

"That resonated with me. He was just so mature, not just on the ice but off it as well."

Lalonde also wasn't worried about the physicality or the skill level overwhelming Ekblad. After all, Ekblad's biggest strength wasn't his body, but rather his mind. He didn't overpower opponents. He nullified them by playing textbook defence. "I remember saying to his dad that there's really zero risk to this," said Lalonde, "because even if we overshot his skill level, his commitment to getting better would narrow that gap."

With Dave Ekblad on board, the next hurdle to overcome was convincing Lisa Ekblad that sending her youngest son away was the best decision for him. As big and mature as Aaron was, he was still her baby. The youngest. It's not easy letting a fourteen-year-old leave the house and live with another family, potentially hours away or in another country. At the same time, she didn't want to stand in the way of an opportunity that could determine his future.

Like any rational mother, she got out a sheet of paper and drew a line down the middle and started to list the pros and cons. "I wrote it all down, the things that I thought would be a potential impact on him," she said, still choking up with emotion while remembering how difficult it was to make the decision. "He and I sat down and I had tears in my eyes as I ran through everything: what about this, what about school, what about your friends, what about loneliness, what about not seeing us and not seeing your brother. And yeah, he convinced me that those were all of my forty-year-old worries, and certainly not a fourteen-year-old's worries. I was just really sad to see my baby go."

As for the actual vetting process, Hockey Canada spent six weeks scouting, interviewing and putting Ekblad through psychological and physical testing. He passed with flying colours. As Branch joked, echoing a familiar comment on Ekblad's maturity: "He probably could have played in the OHL at age fourteen."

THE MAN-CHILD WOULD GET A BODYGUARD. AT LEAST THAT was what Dale Hawerchuk had promised Aaron's mom. "We'll protect him," he'd said. "Don't worry about a thing." So the Barrie Colts traded for Reid McNeill, a 6-foot-4, 215-pound defenceman who was three years older than Ekblad and who had a reputation for dropping the gloves at a moment's notice. The two became defence partners and the message to opposing players was clear: Mess with Ekblad and you'll have to mess with McNeill. Or was it the other way around?

"It was quite evident that he could handle himself," Hawerchuk said of Ekblad. "He was big and strong and just had that look to him. We were like, there's no way this guy's fifteen years old. It was like Aaron was handling Reid and insulating him. If things got out of hand, Aaron would stand up and say, 'That's enough.' And he liked to mix it up too. I think his first fight was with an over-age player and I was thinking, 'Oh boy, here we go.' But he handled himself pretty well."

THE FIRST TIME JASON FORD HEARD THE NAME AARON Ekblad, he reacted how most people would when being told about a twelve-year-old who was going to be the next Nicklas Lidström:

he rolled his eyes and didn't give it another thought. After all, this Ekblad kid was simply that—a kid. And besides, even if he turned out to be something special, he wasn't going to be draft-eligible for another four years. "I heard about him, to be honest with you, through a guy who was working as a Rogers play-by-play guy," remembered Ford. "He was no dummy when it came to hockey. He was calling a game with Ekblad and the only thing he said to me was, 'There was this kid I saw and he never left the ice. He was on the whole game.'"

Two years later, Ford heard Ekblad's name again. This time, he actually paid attention. Just as Ekblad was jumping through the hoops required for exceptional status, the Barrie Colts were preparing for a rebuild after missing the playoffs for the first time in franchise history. That meant nabbing the first overall pick.

"At that time, from our staff, it was a pretty easy consensus that he was going to be the guy," said Ford. "But he still had to go through the exceptional status thing. So we had to keep a pulse on that to see if he was going to be allowed. It was between him and Nick Ritchie. If Aaron didn't get in, Nick was the next best player."

By mid-January, Ekblad's application was accepted. At about the same time, Barrie's rebuild suddenly got serious. The Colts traded their captain, their starting goalie and one of their top scorers all in a matter of days. The moves allowed late-blooming forward Scheifele to get the ice time necessary to score 75 points in 66 games and finish second overall in rookie scoring. But that was about the only bright spot in a season where the Colts managed just fifteen wins—five fewer than the next-worst team—and ended up dead last in the standings. Well, that and picking first overall in the OHL Priority Draft.

"I remember watching [Ekblad] at the Silver Stick in November," said Hawerchuk. "We were a pretty decimated team. It was my first year. We had lost [Alex] Burmistrov and [Kyle]

Clifford to the NHL, so we didn't have a lot. I remember thinking, 'That kid could be our best defenceman *right now.*' And he was fourteen."

Ekblad came into camp looking less like a barely legal rookie and more like a grizzled veteran. "He had a beard," said Ford. "His 'Welcome to the OHL' period? It was like a week."

"He was a man at fifteen, which was crazy," said Scheifele. "But honestly, he was huge for our team." He was also huge for Scheifele. The first time Scheifele met Ekblad was on the first day of training camp, when the players had to compete in a five-kilometre run. They might as well have been the only two players on the track. That was how focused they were on each other. The two took off from the starting line, legs churning around the track with one eye pointed forward and the other eye looking at the person beside them. Neither wanted to give.

"We were neck and neck," said Ekblad. "I think he ended up winning. But that's when I knew he was in good shape. When I saw Mark's work ethic off the ice, it was something I wanted to look up to and follow." It was the first of many one-on-one battles between the two alpha dogs. And it was all in good fun. In Scheifele, Ekblad had found someone who had the drive and determination to get better. They pushed each other constantly, whether it was in the weight room or on the ice.

"He sought out Scheifele," said Hawerchuk. "He wanted to go up against the best all the time. There was a burning desire to be the best and get better every day. Having two guys like that is a coach's dream. You don't have to bark. They push the pace on their own. You just sit back and smile. They made a lot of people better hockey players."

"He was one of the best players in the league," Ekblad said of Scheifele, "so if I could stop him then my thinking was 'how is anyone else going to get around me?' It was my motivation for getting better. I tried to line up against him all the time."

In his first season in the OHL, Ekblad led Colts defencemen with 10 goals and 29 points. By his draft year, he was voted "best shot, hardest shot, best offensive defenceman and best defensive defenceman" in an OHL coaches' poll. "I think the best way to describe him is he's like a general back there," said Hawerchuk. "He wanted to be the general. If things didn't go his way or he got burned, he wasn't happy about it. When you think about it, a guy like Ray Bourque was very similar. He was very good at supporting the puck, had a good shot from the point, was just very solid. Those are guys you build around for a number of years."

BOXERS OR BRIEFS? FLORIDA PANTHERS GM DALE TALLON ISN'T SERIOUSLY interested in what you're wearing underneath your suit. He's just trying to throw you a curveball, make you laugh, see how you can think on your feet. He asks the question of all the players who seem a little too nervous, a little too polished, as if they've memorized all the things they are going to say in the interview. But Ekblad, with his hair styled just so and his suit hugging his impressive frame, was different. He didn't get that question. After all, there was no question as to his NHL potential. "He was pretty cool," said Tallon. "He had the hair and the look. Some kids come in and they look like kids. But Aaron looked like a pro already."

THE PAUSE. IT... NEARLY... KILLED TALLON. WHEN HE WALKED up to the podium to make the first overall pick at the 2014 NHL Entry Draft, Tallon had known for a while what name he was going to say. But he couldn't help but make the prospects—as well as a sold-out crowd that had lustily booed during NHL commissioner Gary Bettman's introduction—sweat a little. "That was more of a shot toward the Philly fans, like let's slow down here and enjoy the process," said Tallon. "What are you doing here? This is supposed to be fun and entertaining, so that's why I kind of did it that way. I'm a smartass."

"Hundred per cent I was left in the dark," said Ekblad, who might have sweated through his suit that day. "There was no way in hell that I knew he was going to pick me. Not until that moment when he said my name."

In his first season in the NHL, Ekblad did what he had previously done in Sun County and in the OHL: he played beyond his years. He scored 12 goals and 39 points as a rookie, logging nearly 22 minutes a night while recording a plus-12 rating, to beat out Gaudreau and Mark Stone for the Calder Memorial Trophy.

"It wasn't like he was great one night and so-so the other night, like most young kids are," said Tallon. "He was good all the time. I think that in itself was exceptional. Not many kids are grounded with a two-hundred-foot game. In every zone, he was in the right position." By the time he was twenty-one years old, Ekblad was already an alternate captain and had logged 227 games.

"They say three hundred games," Tallon said of the amount of time it takes for a defenceman to get comfortable in the NHL. "It's probably true. He's got a chance to be [Shea] Weber-like, that type of player who plays quality minutes, is a reliable guy. That's why he got exceptional status. The package is always solid all the time. I think that in itself is exceptional."

William NYLANDER

TORONTO MAPLE LEAFS
» № 29 «

POSITION	CENTRE
SHOOTS	RIGHT
HEIGHT	6'0"
WEIGHT	191 LB
BORN	MAY 1, 1996
BIRTHPLACE	CALGARY, AB, CAN
DRAFT	2014 TOR, 1ST RD, 8TH PK (8TH OVERALL)

William Nylander (right) races Gustav Nyquist for the puck at the Centennial Classic at Toronto's BMO Field in 2017. The Canadian Press/ Frank Gunn

THE KID WAS A LEGEND EVEN BEFORE HE STEPPED ON the ice. In some ways, he was a legend even before he got out of the car. Picture that you are twelve-year-old Zach Pard as he arrives at hockey tryouts for Team Maryland in the fall of 2008. As you're getting your equipment out of the trunk, a luxury SUV pulls into the parking lot beside you. The driver's side door opens and out walks Michael Nylander. You know who this is because your family has owned season tickets to the Washington Capitals for almost ten years and you were just saying that getting a veteran like Nylander was going to make the Caps a real Cup contender.

But wait—who's that coming out of the passenger side door? Is that... No way, it can't be... Holy crap, it is... Nicklas Backstrom?!? He was the Caps' fourth overall pick last year. He's a rookie, but he's supposed to be really, really good and will help turn Alex Ovechkin—who is your favourite player, by the way—into a sixty-goal scorer. Then the rear door opens and you see this short, skinny kid with clear blue eyes and floppy blond hair, who's clearly younger than you, and you're thinking, *What is going on right now? Who is this that's trying out for our team?*

That was how Zach Pard first met William Nylander. And although Nylander insists getting chauffeured to tryouts by an NHL forward who had played more than nine hundred games in the NHL and another who would become one of the league's best playmaking centres was "normal," it was anything but for those around him. After all, it's not normal that your teammates are asking your dad for his signature. "It was a huge deal to me," said Pard. "At the end of the year, I said, 'Mr. Nylander, I don't usually do this, but I don't know if I'll see you again. Can I have your autograph?'"

There are a lot of those kinds of stories over the years. Like the time when Ovechkin came over for Thanksgiving dinner or when William would play Ping-Pong with Backstrom or when his father would call a few of his NHL teammates if his son was short a few players for a game of road hockey. "Now we understand how special it was," said William. "Back then, it was just how it was. You didn't think about it or whether other guys got to see NHL guys or whatever. It was normal. It's just how we grew up."

William Nylander looks like a typical Swede, with blond hair and blue eyes, but as he developed, he became a hybrid player, combining North American and European styles of play. Photo courtesy of Daniel Lackner

Michael Nylander scored 679 points in 920 NHL games, but he's logged so many miles that his hockey career is straight out of a road-tripping Johnny Cash song. He played everywhere, man: Hartford, Calgary, Tampa Bay, Chicago, Washington, Boston, New York, Springfield, Mass., Grand Rapids, Rochester, Sweden, Finland, Russia, Switzerland and even Italy. Often, William and the rest of the family went along for the ride. For example, look at William's place of birth. He is Canadian, having been born in Calgary when his father was playing for the Flames. But he moved to the United States two years later after Michael was traded to the Tampa Bay Lightning. And Michael was playing in Chicago two years after that.

William was brought up in the nomadic lifestyle of a hockey journeyman, packing up and moving at a moment's notice, sleeping in hotels and with friends of friends, calling parts of the United States and Sweden home, but never really setting down roots in one particular place. "My kids never asked why are we here and not there or anything, they just enjoyed everywhere they've been," said his father. "They got used to it. They were really happy to be wherever we were, whether it was Chicago or New York or Sweden. It was like taking their bag and playing for another team. They saw how it goes in the NHL and were used to that kind of living."

Two things happened because of that kind of childhood: the first is that Nylander, whose accent is a blend from growing up in New York, Maryland and Stockholm, does not play like a prototypical European or North American. He skates and stickhandles with the patience and precision of most Swedish players. And yet the Swedes have at times considered him too selfish of a shooter to truly be one of their own.

"I think that he's definitely a hybrid player," said Anders Sorensen, a close family friend who has coached Nylander in both Chicago and Sweden. "A lot of his skating and whatnot is attributed to playing over there and being taught a certain way. But the mentality is different than the European-influenced player. He wants the puck, he wants to be *the guy*—where sometimes I found that European players would rather take the back seat and let other people score."

Another thing that happened: in watching his father experience success and failure at the highest levels, Nylander developed a thick skin that has prepared him for the inevitable ups and downs that every hockey player faces. He has seen his father score 83 points on a line with Jaromir Jagr. But he's also seen him bounce around from team to team and league to league and country to country looking for his next job. Nylander was fourteen years old when his father went headfirst into the boards and broke his neck in an AHL game.

A year later, he watched his father go through painful rehab from spinal fusion surgery and try out for the Philadelphia Flyers. He did not make the team, but he also did not give up. He just found another place to play, playing hockey wherever he could. The lesson for William was that talent alone takes you so far. To play professionally, it takes hard work and perseverance.

William, who scored 61 points in his first full season with the Maple Leafs and followed it up with another 61 points in 2017–18, is a product of that perseverance. He calls his upbringing normal—and maybe it was for him—but it was also special. "We would be with him in the locker room, so we would see the NHL lifestyle," William said of him and his brother. "I think I learned a lot through my dad, him being in the league and knowing what it takes. It taught me and my brother a lot, just how to prepare."

THE HOCKEY GAME WAS WHAT YOU WOULD EXPECT FROM THE MITE LEVEL. There was no structure, no organization, no positional play. As the puck moved up and down the ice, a pack of six-year-olds moved along with it, a giant blob of sticks and skates. Except for one.

Nylander stayed away from the pack and waited for the puck to pop out his way. It was an unexpected level of hockey intelligence at an age level where some kids were confused as to what net they were shooting on. What happened next was equally unexpected. Once he had the puck, Nylander didn't skate up the ice—he turned around and started to skate back to his own end. The coaches and parents thought he was confused. "Wrong way! Wrong way! You're going the wrong way!"

Nylander ignored them. Instead he circled behind his own net and stopped. He then left the puck there and skated up the sideboards, his stick on the ice in a position to receive a pass that never came. "He was waiting for the defenceman to pick it up and break it out, but nobody knows what's going on so nobody picks the puck up," said Michael Nylander, laughing. "But that's what they do in the NHL."

The problem? He was six years old.

IT STARTED EARLY. VERY EARLY, IN FACT. SOME HOCKEY PARents like to joke that their kids were skating before they were walking. For William, he practically learned how to walk while wearing skates. "He had the skates on in the house, because we had carpet in some places," said Michael Nylander. "He would be walking around on them. Where there was hardwood floor, we told him he couldn't stand there because it would scratch the floors, so he was crawling on the hardwood floors and then walking on the carpet."

Growing up, all William and his brother Alex, who is two years younger, wanted to do was play hockey. Of course they did. Their father played in the NHL, which meant they had the kind of closed-door access that most kids—and let's be honest, most adults—could only dream about. Their father's teammates, whether they were Alex Ovechkin or Nicklas Backstrom, were not NHL stars to them. They were friends who always seemed to be at the house hanging out because they were young bachelors and Michael Nylander had a reputation as the best chef in the NHL. Seriously, his spaghetti carbonara was better than his wrist shot.

"He's a phenomenal cook," said Backstrom, who was new to the country and still a teenager at the time. "He was standing in the kitchen from 2 p.m. to 7 p.m., just cooking all day. I was not living with them, but I was over there all the time, playing Ping-Pong and picking up the kids from practices sometimes. I was playing with the kids and Michael was cooking for us. It was perfect."

Having a dad who was in the NHL had an obvious effect on William and Alex. The life of an NHLer became so ingrained in their heads that when the boys used to go outside to play road hockey, they would first put on their suits and ties because that's what their father did when he went to play hockey. "That was their road trip," said Michael. "Then they'd go and play the game." Even when playing mini-sticks in the basement, whoever was playing in net would pause the game to squeeze water into his face like the goalies did on their father's team. "They were imitating us at a really young age in all kinds of ways," said Michael.

There were other influences. Michael Nylander is the first person to tell you that he wasn't always around for his six kids. How could he be? Up until 2014–15, when William was eighteen years old, Michael was still playing professionally in Sweden. He was either travelling to games, or because he was a journeyman who never lasted more than four years in one place, he was sometimes playing in one city while his wife Camilla and their six kids lived somewhere else.

"I was on the road all the time," said Michael Nylander. "I was always away somewhere and [William and Alex] were always playing somewhere else. There was always somebody picking up one of the kids and my wife took the other. There were maybe only five, six, eight times a year where you could watch them play."

The hockey community is a tight family, no matter what city you are living in. Coaches, convenors and others opened up their homes to the travelling Nylanders. When in Chicago, they spent time with Anders Sorensen, who would become William's long-time coach. When they moved to Maryland, they lived on and off with Bob Weiss, whose spacious five-bedroom home suddenly seemed cramped after the Nylanders unpacked. "They arrived with something like twenty-four hockey bags full of clothes, if you can imagine," said Bob Weiss. "My wife will jokingly tell you that one reason she allowed the Nylanders to stay was because he said he would cook every night. My wife said, 'Done deal. You can stay as long as you want.'"

William never really stayed in one spot long enough to call it home. He was two years old when his dad was traded from Calgary to Tampa Bay. Two years later, his dad was traded to Chicago. By the time he arrived in Washington in 2002–03, the six-year-old was on his fourth NHL city. "He bounced around a lot, so he had to be guarded," said Team Maryland head coach Dan Houck. "He didn't know where he was going to be twenty-four hours from the next day. You're talking about a kid whose parents might not be home for the night or whatever, and Willie would be in charge of his brother and four sisters at age eleven. He was very mature, very responsible."

William Nylander grabs the puck while playing for Team Maryland. Photo courtesy of Daniel Lackner

By then, Nylander had already begun to cultivate a reputation as a slick-skating forward who was usually playing a year up. "Honestly back then, even at a young age, his puck-handling ability, his skating ability, his compete level set him apart," said Rob Keegan, one of William's earliest coaches with Team Maryland. "His skating seemed effortless."

"I remember I was over at his house one day and we were just shooting pucks and having a good time," said Pard. "And then his brother came out. We're all in the garage ripping pucks and they're going bar down and picking corners."

Nylander was always good enough to play up an age level. But heading into his first season of full-contact hockey, there were some concerns about whether a player who was so slight and so small could take a hit. Dan Houck had an easy way to answer that. At the start of training camp, the players performed a "gauntlet drill" where the entire team lined up against the boards and one by one a player had to try to skate through the mass of bodies. "One of our players broke his clavicle," said Pard. Nylander fared slightly better.

"He was tiny," said Houck. "He weighed like 70 pounds and some of these kids he's playing against were 130 pounds. And, I mean, this kid would get absolutely flattened and he'd just bounce back up like a rubber band and go again."

Houck was an interesting coach. Pard described him as "hard-nosed," the kind of person who wouldn't take crap from anyone and who expected his players to act the same. Houck knew that Nylander was offensively gifted—he scored 25 goals and 51 points in 28 games that year—but he also knew that scoring goals was only a part of what made a player and a team successful. He needed Nylander to play as hard without the puck as he did with it.

Team Maryland was the 2007–2008 peewee champion. William Nylander is in the front row, second from left. Photo courtesy of Daniel Lackner

And so, following a one-sided loss where the team hadn't sacrificed their bodies enough in blocking shots, the coach showed up to the next day's practice with a basket full of tennis balls. Houck stood on the blue line and instructed a player to skate toward him. He then took out a tennis ball and wound up. "Now block it!" he shouted. "If you missed the tennis ball, he used the puck," said Pard. "He definitely did not like cutting corners in any way."

While this was going on, Michael Nylander was having his worst season in the NHL. On a Capitals team that was trending young—a twenty-two-year-old Ovechkin had won the Hart Memorial Trophy as the league MVP and Backstrom, who was nineteen, had just scored 88 points—Nylander's best days were long gone. He finished with 9 goals and 22 points in 72 games. It would be the last time he played in the NHL.

The following season, Washington sent him to Detroit, where he was assigned to the minors in Grand Rapids, Michigan, before leaving to play in Finland. The rest of the family needed more stability, so they moved back to Chicago, where William was reunited with Sorensen. "Anders is a very, very special guy and he's really knowledgeable," said Michael Nylander. "Of course, when your kids get to have a coach like that around when they're so young, it's a unique opportunity. He's done so well with my boys."

Sorensen is a few years younger than Michael Nylander. They grew up not far from each other in Sweden. If Houck was the coach who tried to add a layer of grit to Nylander's game, Sorensen was the one who tapped into Nylander's Swedish roots. Don't worry about dumping and chasing after the puck. Instead, hang onto it; reverse it back to your end if you have to. Control the pace. Don't be afraid to slow down the game.

For Nylander, it was a dream scenario. Not only was he now playing for a coach who wasn't blasting tennis balls at his body, but he was also playing on a team where he wasn't the only player destined for the NHL. Nick Schmaltz and Christian Dvorak were his linemates with the Chicago Mission team that became a powerhouse. "It was one of those deals where, 'Okay, we need a goal, put that line out there,'" said Sorensen.

Nylander scored 34 goals and 61 points in 29 games and led the Chicago Mission U-14 team to the USA Hockey national championships, where they lost in the final to a Belle Tire team that had Dylan Larkin, Zach Werenski and Kyle Connor. "We lost 6–5," said Sorensen. "We were down 5–2 and we got two straight five-on-threes. If I remember right, Nick scored and then William scored and we scored another to make it 5–5."

In another tournament, the Mission went up against a Toronto Marlboros team that had Connor McDavid, Robby Fabbri and Josh Ho-Sang. The Mission more than held their own, a sign that Nylander was developing at pace with the best players in his age group. "That was the first time I realized just how good he was," said Sorensen. "William was every bit as good or even better in my mind. I told Michael, 'This kid's the real thing. He is probably the top ten in the world.'" And then, of course, they were on the move again.

> I've known him since he was ten or eleven. The talent has been there the whole time. He's probably the most talented player I have ever worked with. He's special. William is close to Erik Karlsson. He's in the same ballpark for talent. It was really interesting to coach him, because his skill level is so high there. When I see a guy like William Nylander, he's the top, top, top guy in the draft for me. I would have picked him much earlier than eighth. I really like that type of player. They can make a big difference. And people love to pay and go see them. It's entertainment to see these types of guys.
>
> **— ANDERS FORSBERG,**
> **MODO coach**

IN 2011, MICHAEL NYLANDER HAD ALL BUT DECIDED HIS NHL career was over, so he returned to Europe where the travel was lighter, the hockey was less physical and there was a spot for him. But really, his two sons wanted to return to their roots. "I think for some reason they wanted to play a little bit in Sweden and try it out here," said Michael Nylander. "They had a really good time when they came over and played for some good teams and some good coaches as well."

From a language and cultural perspective, the transition went smoothly. "Home is Sweden," said William. "That's where all the family is. We were back there every summer." It also helped that Sorensen decided to join them, taking a job with Södertälje SK so he could coach William. And yet there was still an adjustment.

With a style inspired by the protagonist in the Zelda video games, the blond-haired and blue-eyed Nylander might look like a prototypical Swede. To the untrained eye, it might even seem like he learned to stickhandle from watching video of the Sedin twins. But when Nylander arrived in Sweden, he was a lone wolf in sheep's clothing. "He was, like, a *shooter* and everybody was just like, 'Who does this guy think he is?'" said Dmytro Timashov.

"The North American part of him was just being self-ish, and what I mean by that is he was actually shooting," said Rikard Grönborg, who coached Nylander at the World Junior Championship. "In Sweden we're always looking for a pass. If you look at our centres and defencemen especially, we have a lot of good passers out here. Where he would come on the ice and would be thinking shoot first and pass second. To me, it was refreshing to see a player like that who was actually wired a little differently than the other players we had."

Of course, it must be mentioned that Grönborg went to college at St. Cloud State in Minnesota and spent a decade coaching in the United States before returning home to Sweden. If anyone could see the value in Nylander's style, it would be him. Others, however, were sometimes confused by it. To some, Nylander was a me-first player, more interested in padding his own stats than playing the team game. He always wanted the puck. He always wanted to be the one taking the shot. Maybe that wouldn't have been a problem had he been born and developed in Sweden. But the perception of him when he arrived was that he was the son of an NHLer acting like he was also a star.

"You know how it is when your dad is playing in the NHL and now you're good; there can be a jealousy factor from other players there," said Sorensen. "Personally, I thought he adjusted very quickly. The first couple of games he had a rough time, because he's sixteen and playing against twenty-year-olds. But five, six games into it, he really started to find his ground. We played Brynäs IF in the playoffs and they had Elias Lindholm [a fifth overall pick of the Carolina Hurricanes in 2013]. Nylander dominated against them to the point where he made Lindholm look like an average player."

The bigger rink suited Nylander. He was always a terrific skater and loved to hang onto the puck and now he had so much more room to operate. For opposing players, it was like trying to swat at a fly. He buzzed around, darting this way and that, using the open ice like his own playground.

"I know a lot of people in Toronto want to compare Mitch Marner to Patrick Kane, but I actually think William is more like [Kane] in how he reads and reacts and changes the pace of the game," said Sorensen. "It used to drive me crazy as a coach. But he's just so confident. It's almost like he's trying to goad people in. And then when the D commits to him, that's when he uses a cut pass or blows by a guy. That's very, very similar to Kane."

At first blush, Nylander plays like a typical European. He likes to cut back and circle with the puck, taking his time to find holes in the defence. But once his mind is made up, he attacks. "I would say he's a hybrid for sure," Sorensen said. "He can break the game open because of his skill and his hockey sense, but you're never going to ask him to be the first guy in the corner."

Without the puck, Nylander was like most sixteen-year-old skilled players: invisible. He didn't backcheck. When he did, he was just going through the motions or delivering an Oscar-worthy performance to show how fatigued he was. "He would fake being tired," said Anders Forsberg. "In the beginning, he showed everyone, 'Oh, I'm too tired to do this backcheck or do this thing.'"

Forsberg still laughs at the memory of a totally gassed Nylander barely making it to the bench as the opposing team was rushing the other way, only to realize that the puck had been turned over. With that, he found a second wind and rejoined the rush, skating at top speed. "He would look totally dead on the backcheck—skating like he would hopefully get to the bench—and then all of a sudden he is 100 per cent fresh?" said Forsberg. "As you stand there on the bench, you're like, 'What is this!?!' A normal coach would be freaking out. But afterward you're laughing because he scored."

Although Forsberg saw the potential in a player like Nylander, he was realistic about having a sixteen-year-old in the lineup. "He was the most skilled guy on the team right from day one," said Forsberg. "The biggest problem was that we weren't so good as a team. We spent too much time in the defensive zone. So that was a problem. And he wasn't strong enough for it at the time. If we were a better team, it would have been perfect for him."

Nylander scored only 1 goal and had 6 assists in 22 games for MODO in 2013–14. The lack of offence was mostly due to ice time. He couldn't be trusted to play top-line minutes. "I was like, 'Oh, boy, this is not a guy that follows the system,'" said Forsberg. "A couple of the older guys were irritated and some coaches too. If he had a chance to get the puck, he would put in 100 per cent effort. But if it was an ordinary backcheck or a battle along the boards that he had no chance to win, he put in 60 per cent effort and he would wait for someone else to do the job there."

The one-sided effort was a reason why Nylander was loaned to Rögle BK and Södertälje SK, which at the time were playing in a division that was lower than MODO. "It wasn't that he couldn't play. It was that the coach wasn't using him the right way," said Sorensen, perhaps ignoring the fact that the coach was trying to win games and not develop junior-aged players. "It happens a lot with younger players. You have this ultra-talented player and you're using him on the fourth line? I remember telling Michael to bring him [to Södertälje]. He can play and be the guy."

With Södertälje SK, Nylander showcased the skills that have been on display ever since he made the jump to the NHL. Playing on a team with David Pastrnak, Nylander scored 11 goals and 19 points in 17 games. "I remember our coach came to us one morning and said a player from MODO was going to be loaned to us and his name was William Nylander," said Dan Iliakis, a defenceman with Södertälje. "You didn't know what to expect, but there was definitely a buzz around him. He was a huge boost for us."

Still, it was a weird season. The constant moving around—Nylander played for three different teams in his draft year—and complaints about his defensive game and perceived selfishness earned him some harsh criticism heading into the 2014 NHL Entry Draft. Red Line Report, a North American scouting service, described him as the "most skilled player in the draft, but a massive diva."

The Maple Leafs selected Nylander with the eighth overall pick, which today looks like a steal. "I was afraid that he was not going to be there," the Leafs' European-based scout Thommie Bergman told Postmedia News. "I thought he was going to go at five. He's extremely talented. He has to be a little bit stronger, but his hands, his skating, everything is high level."

The following year, Nylander returned to MODO, where he scored 8 goals and 20 points in 21 games. But by January, the team was on its way to a losing season and relegation to Sweden's second division. Forsberg was fired. Not long after, Nylander joined the Maple Leafs' AHL affiliate for the second half of the season, finishing with 14 goals and 32 points in 37 games.

WILLIAM: "I WAS OPEN—HOW COME YOU DIDN'T GIVE ME THE PUCK?"
Michael: "I had the better handle on the puck and you weren't really open."
William: "Then why didn't you score? You had an open net. Score a goal."

THERE ARE SIGNS ALL OVER THE HOCKEY ARENA WARNING parents to not get too involved, reminding everyone that this is a game and that these are kids. *Watch. Be respectful.* Most importantly, *Keep your distance.* It's a familiar message to any hockey parent. But Michael Nylander wasn't just any hockey parent. He couldn't just watch. And he certainly couldn't keep his distance. With his oldest son playing in a men's league in Sweden, Michael Nylander had to live out a dream and make a comeback.

"That was a fantastic time, of course," said Michael Nylander. "Playing with your own kids, that was never in my head until I was close to the situation and it happened. Of course, it was a little bit different when you normally drive to the rink and drop William or Alex off. Now, we were there together in the locker room and then on the ice. We had our arguments as teammates do. It was fun. It was great."

Michael Nylander never thought he was going to be the Swedish Gordie Howe when he moved back to Stockholm. But he still wanted to play. At thirty-nine, he still felt like he had more to give. He wasn't capable of playing for MODO, where William started the 2013–14 season. But when the team loaned William to Södertälje and then Rögle, Michael came along for the ride. Quite literally.

The two drove to practice together, often talking about things that they should do together as linemates in the game. If those conversations were fun, the ones on the ride back home were definitely more interesting. They bickered, not as father and son, but as teammates. Michael Nylander called it the best two years of his career: "To play on the same team, it was pretty special. It was unbelievable to go to practice together."

On the ice and off it, they were each other's biggest supporters and critics. Michael was at the very end of a lengthy professional career, his legs no longer capable of doing what his mind wanted. William was at the beginning of his, all flash and dash but lacking in experience. Chemistry was never a problem. But when things did not go right, they let each other hear it.

No question, their relationship was unusual. But for William, it was as normal as playing Ping-Pong in the basement with Nicklas Backstrom or having Alex Ovechkin over to the house for Thanksgiving dinner. He was used to it, even if the sight of his father and him side by side on the bench became a photo-op. "It's funny because at the rink they have all these signs for youth hockey," said Anders Sorensen. "One said, *No Parents Allowed on the Bench*. Someone took a picture of it—with the two of them sitting there."

TODAY, WILLIAM NYLANDER IS NOT HIS FATHER'S TEAMMATE. HE is no longer known as the son of an NHLer, but rather one of the league's rising young talents. He's paving his own route, becoming his own type of player. And yet he can't really escape the past.

At the 2017 world championship, Nylander found himself on a line with Nicklas Backstrom. It was like the old days, except they weren't using mini-sticks and Nylander was no longer in the back seat of the car. "I knew that I was going to play with him on the national team and that's actually one reason why I wanted to go," said Backstrom. "It was great. He's a great player and we had chemistry right away. It made everything easier." Nylander led the team to a gold medal with 7 goals and 14 points, earning MVP honours in the process. "When it's time to shine, he shines. And when it's time to relax and recover, he's pretty laid back. He's going to have a great career."

No one called him selfish during the tournament. No one said he was playing like a diva or that he was shooting too much or pretending to be tired on the backcheck—although there were some complaints that he was hitting too hard. After Sweden had won gold in a shootout against Canada, Nylander jumped over the boards and sprinted down the ice toward Henrik Lundqvist. He meant to embrace the goalie in a celebratory hug, but in his excitement he ended up tackling Lundqvist to the ground, injuring him.

As some joked, that was the North American side of him coming out again. "You see the smile on his face and the pure joy of him playing," said Rikard Grönborg. "He just loves the game. Everything is so grave these days and there's so much pressure on these guys. For me it's so refreshing to see that."

Jack EICHEL

BUFFALO SABRES
» № 15 «

POSITION	CENTRE
SHOOTS	RIGHT
HEIGHT	6′2″
WEIGHT	206 LB
BORN	OCTOBER 28, 1996
BIRTHPLACE	NORTH CHELMSFORD, MA, USA
DRAFT	2015 BUF, 1ST RD, 2ND PK (2ND OVERALL)

Buffalo Sabres' Jack Eichel prepares for a faceoff against the Tampa Bay Lightning in 2015. AP Photo/Chris O'Meara, File

IF YOU WANT TO GET INSIDE THE MIND OF JACK EICHEL, go to his parents' home in North Chelmsford, Massachusetts, where on the back of his bedroom door there used to hang a poster of Tom Brady. When he went to bed it would be the last thing he saw before closing his eyes. Eichel didn't necessarily dream about playing in the NFL, but he did dream about becoming great. That's why he put up a poster of a five-time Super Bowl champion quarterback. And it's why Kobe Bryant and Sidney Crosby and several others later appeared on what would become a revolving door of motivation and inspiration.

Sometimes it wasn't an athlete on his door. Sometimes, it wasn't even someone famous. "Maybe it was a picture of somebody who was the same age as me that I thought was better than me—who I thought I should be better than," said Eichel. "There were small things that I did to motivate myself. I watched a lot of videos, a lot of things, about other great athletes or great people, whether it was football players or whatever. I think I'm still like that, whether I'm watching a documentary on Kobe Bryant or something on Tom Brady or players in the NHL."

Eichel, the Buffalo Sabres centre who was selected with the second overall pick in the 2015 NHL Entry Draft, scored 57 points in 61 games in his second season (and 64 points in 67 games in 2017–18). It was a points-per-game pace that put him just outside the top ten in the league. And yet, when he returned home after the season was complete, he went looking for motivation and inspiration. This time it didn't come from his bedroom door. Instead, he called up Boston Bruins forward Brad Marchand, who had finished in the top five in goals and points, and asked if he could tag along with him to the gym.

"You'd be pretty surprised at how hard he works," Eichel said of Marchand, who is eight years older and three inches shorter than him. "It was eye-opening. It pushes you and makes you want to get better and makes you want to work hard. This is my job and I think I have a lot to prove. I'm willing to do whatever it takes."

Brian Burke, the loquacious speaker and Calgary Flames president, once told USA *Today* of Eichel, "Even if you were an alien from a spaceship who had never seen hockey, and you watched this kid, you would say, 'Good lord, that's a talented athlete.'" The talent comes naturally for Eichel, who learned to skate when he was three years old. But his work ethic comes just as naturally. He has always been a doer more than a dreamer—helped along by that little bit of talent, obviously.

"A bit of talent? You knew right away he has a bit of a talent, but you didn't know any of this other stuff," said Eichel's father, Bob. "He wouldn't go to sleepovers if he had a game the next day. I'd say, 'Jack, it's a squirt game.' He didn't care. He would come home from school and shoot a hundred pucks, do a hundred push-ups, sit-ups."

Bob Eichel said he doesn't know where his son got his powerful yet effortless stride. It sure wasn't from his father. Bob played all kinds of sports growing up, including hockey, and considers himself decent enough at pretty much all of them. But he wasn't a natural. He didn't play in the NHL or Division-1 on a college scholarship. Growing up in Melrose, Massachusetts, which used to be known as Hockeytown, USA ("before Detroit stole the term," he said), Bob didn't even make his high school hockey team. "I played everything: football, baseball, basketball, ran track. But I wasn't anything special," said Bob Eichel. "Not like him."

WHILE HIS SON WAS AT THE GYM, BOB EICHEL WAS AT WORK, having pulled another twelve-hour shift at F.W. Webb plumbing company in Lowell, Massachusetts. He is the sort of hands-on manager who is rarely at his desk to answer the phone, let alone sit down for lunch. When asked on a July evening if he had been enjoying the summer and taken any time off to go on vacation, he cut the question short and answered back, "What vacation? I work from six to six every day."

His wife, Anne, who is a registered nurse at Boston Medical Center, is the same way. She was back at work at 7 a.m. the morning after her son was drafted by the Sabres. She is also not home on this night, because she's working the night shift this week. In other words, Jack might not have received any natural athleticism from his parents. But there's no question that he's wearing their blue-collar genes when it comes to work ethic.

"That's why I am who I am right now," said Eichel. "My mom's almost sixty and she gets up every day at 4 a.m. and goes to work for twelve hours. She drives into Boston, and it's not like she does an easy job either. My dad's the same way. He's working harder now than when he was twenty, so I think that's where I got it. It was the kind of thing where your parents come home and you're sitting on the couch watching TV and you get that sarcastic remark from your dad and it makes you almost feel guilty. I think I started to grow into the type of person where I felt guilty if I wasn't working hard."

It's funny how it works, but it's often the students who are already getting an A-plus in class who take advantage of the extra credit assignments. That was Eichel. His mother used to say that as a toddler "he skates better than he walks." But natural ability only takes you so far. Lots of kids have been naturally talented and lots of kids have looked like they were born with skates on their feet. Some have even coasted by on that natural talent and become good NHL hockey players. But Eichel didn't want to just become good.

When he was a kid, he would tell everyone that he was going to play Division-1 in college and then play in the NHL. He told family members, friends, teachers and whomever he happened to be talking to. "He told everybody in the world," said Bob. "I've been in the line in coffee shops and teachers have come up to me and said, 'He told me in the fourth grade that he was going to play in the NHL. Kids laughed at him'—and the teacher actually said to me—'but I knew he would.' She had never seen him play hockey in her entire life."

As a child, Jack Eichel told everyone that he was going to play Division-1 in college and then play in the NHL. Photo courtesy of the Eichel family

What had the teacher seen in him? The same thing Eichel saw when he looked at the poster of Tom Brady: desire to be the best. As his father said, he did the things that other kids wouldn't do. Things like going to bed early so he wouldn't be tired for the game the next day. Things like riding his bike to the gym while others took the car. Things like playing up several levels, even though it meant he didn't get to play as much or score as often, because he wanted a challenge. He was driven to be the best. Possessed by it. Teachers saw it. So did coaches, scouts and teammates. It was inspiring.

EICHEL COMES FROM NORTH CHELMSFORD—NOT Chelmsford. If you don't know the difference between the two, there is apparently a local priest who will set you straight. That's what happened to Bob Eichel when he first moved there. At the time, he and his soon-to-be-wife believed they were settling down in a cul-de-sac in the suburbs north of Boston, where the houses were bigger, the streets were quieter, and the people were more educated and affluent. *The good life*, he thought to himself. "I told the priest, 'I made it. I got out of the city. I'm living in Chelmsford,'" said Bob Eichel. "And he goes, 'Buddy, you live in North Chelmsford. That's the working-class area.' Chelmsford was the higher-end area."

There are no train tracks separating Chelmsford from North Chelmsford. Both towns actually share a high school and are run by the same government. But there is a divide between the two towns that is apparent to anyone living in either area. It's not exactly like the Greasers and Socs in *The Outsiders*, but it's close. As Eichel's best friend and Chelmsford native Dan Ferri explains, "North Chelmsford were always kind of the tougher kids."

The working-class spirit of the city served Jack well. He was always a little rougher around the edges, a little hard-headed. He was the kid who climbed out of his crib at ten months old, who had so much energy that his parents took literally every knick-knack off the shelves because little Jack would break them. "We could have knick-knacks on the table with our daughter," said Bob Eichel. "Once Jack came around, everything had to come off. He was a lunatic. He was a good kid, but he just had a lot of energy."

When Jack was four, his parents signed him up for a learn-to-skate program. Except Jack didn't want to learn how to skate. He wanted to learn how to play hockey with the older kids at the other end of the rink. "They told him he had to learn to skate because you had to do that first," said Bob Eichel. "He was only four. He said no and went right down to the older kids to learn to play hockey. They didn't kick him out. He was better than those kids anyway."

It wasn't that Eichel was always better than every other kid. He wasn't. But he made himself better. Eichel once read a magazine story about how Tom Brady did one hundred push-ups and one hundred sit-ups every day. So Eichel did that every day too. He heard that Sidney Crosby took one hundred shots. Eichel did that too. "Before we'd drive to Andover to work out with Mike Boyle, he'd be at home riding the bike for like an hour," said Ferri. "It was crazy. At a young age, he was just such a workhorse. He was never talking or socializing in the gym. It was work."

Eichel and Ferri played hockey together when they were younger, before Eichel outgrew his peers. "He was always a step ahead of kids," said Ferri. "I think everyone kind of knew he was going places. I remember my dad telling me when I was younger that he was going to the NHL. I remember watching his first game with the Sabres. We streamed it. My dad bought this box, because he knew we were going to want to watch all his games and stuff and we don't get all the channels out here, but it was terrible quality. Jack scored and it was just so surreal to me. He was actually out there in a Buffalo Sabres jersey and scoring a goal in the NHL. A guy from here."

A few years earlier, the same guy had been feeding Ferri passes, making him look good, like he might be joining Eichel in the NHL one day too. A favourite memory when the old friends are together is the "famous" squirt championship final where Eichel won the faceoff in overtime and passed it back to Ferri for the winning goal. "I just let it go and it went in," said Ferri. "It was nuts. I remember getting absolutely mauled. We still talk about that goal."

Several years later, Ferri set up his buddy off the ice when Eichel returned to high school just in time for the prom, but without a date. "He actually went with one of my date's friends," said Ferri. "I wouldn't say growing up that the girls were lining up for him, but the tables have definitely turned around a little since then."

Growing up, there were limitations to what Eichel wanted to achieve. As much as he wanted to play and get better, his parents didn't put him in summer hockey or send him to private skating or skills coaches until he was thirteen years old. There wasn't any money for it. And even if there was, his parents were careful about giving him too much. Besides, why pay for ice time when there were perfectly good ponds around every street corner? All you had to do was grab your shovel and your stick and skates.

"We all shovelled," said Bob. "There was one [pond] in Chelsea where the guy shovelled it and put out two regulation nets. That was one of the nice ones. But there were shit ones too. [Jack] and I would be out there at all hours. It would be a pain in the ass. I remember when he was four years old, we couldn't even see each other passing the puck back and forth. It was pitch black on the pond. But he wouldn't go back in. I was freezing my ass off. It was a February day. I'll never forget it."

Jack and his father learned to deal with the cold. And they learned to deal with the poor lighting caused by a rolling mist that usually arrived around suppertime. They even learned to deal with an ice surface that was so bumpy it was like driving on the shoulder of a highway. The shoddy conditions made Jack a better player. He was forced to trust his instincts, feeling for the puck rather than looking for it, having to balance more on his edges lest he tripped and fell and smacked his head on the hard ground. "Jack was the best pond hockey player I ever saw," said his father. "He was skating with all the bumps and everything."

In the summer, the routine was different. Eichel lived on a cul-de-sac, which meant he had half a rink just outside his door. Deking a tennis ball underneath parked cars and bouncing it off the curb, he was out there on his rollerblades even more than he was on the pond. "Every time I hung out with him he was doing something productive, like rollerblading or shooting pucks," said Cameron MacDonald, a childhood friend. "We all knew that he was better than us, but he would never shove it in our face. That one year, nationals were in Buffalo and they did a [shootout] competition afterward. He did a spin-o-rama to beat the goalie and won the competition. That was pretty absurd for an eleven-year-old. Our jaws dropped a little bit. He definitely knew what he was doing. He was confident. He knew he could pull it off. I would never try that. I'd probably fall over or something."

"The thing that stood out to me about Jack was really just his unconditional passion and love for hockey," said Cameron's father Blaise MacDonald. "He just seemed like this young boy with curly hair and a big smile on his face whenever he could be around his teammates and playing the game that he loved. If given the opportunity, he would play hockey twenty-six hours a day."

He wasn't just playing. He was working. Some kids take slapshots at the net, aiming for top corners and trying to ring it off the posts. Eichel took the shots that no one practises. One summer, it was just backhands all day long, over and over again, until his wrists became arthritic. "When he was thirteen years old, he said to me, 'I need to work on my first step,'" remembered his dad. "I'm going, 'How did you get that one?' But he would listen to all the pro hockey players and maybe that's where he gets all his ideas."

Eventually, it wasn't just his backhand or his first step. According to Eichel, his entire game needed to get better. So he decided to play against men.

***

DAN FERRI KNEW HIS GOOD BUDDY JACK WAS A BIT OBSESSIVE WHEN IT came to training. But it was still surprising when Eichel showed up to the beach house Ferri's family rented in New Hampshire with his hockey bag full of equipment. "Seriously? I invited him up to the beach for a weekend vacation and he's going to the rink?" Well, not exactly. Eichel put on his gear. But he didn't go to the rink. Instead, in the summer's heat, he walked down to the beach in everything but his skates and started shooting pucks off a plastic board into the water. "He had on his helmet, his gloves, shoulder pads, pants, all his equipment," said Ferri. "It was hysterical. Everyone was looking at him like, 'What is this kid doing?' We were in tears laughing."

THE DIFFERENCE BETWEEN A THIRTEEN-YEAR-OLD AND A seventeen-year-old is substantial. In those four years of development, your body undergoes some crazy changes. Your face starts breaking out in pimples, you grow body hair in places that used to be totally bare, and your voice cracks and then drops an octave or two lower. You literally go from being a boy to a man. Eichel was not yet in high school when Chris Masters suggested he play for the Boston Junior Bruins. Eichel was that good. He had already won a state championship and was scoring practically every time he stepped on the ice. He needed a challenge. More than that, he needed to fail.

Jack Eichel plays for the Junior Bruins. Photo courtesy of the Eichel family

"I was probably a little over my head," said Eichel. "And that's probably a good thing. I always tried to challenge myself and I always thought if I was a step ahead of everyone else, pushing myself harder, that when I went to play against guys my own age I'd be that much better. I learned a lot that year. I grew up fast. You have to. You're in the eighth grade and you're in a locker room with guys who are already out of high school."

Chris Masters and his older brother Peter have spent more than a dozen years running the U-18 and premier teams for the Boston Bruins. Both played together at Boston College, where Chris was a two-way centre and Peter was a stay-at-home defence-man who was a finalist for the Hobey Baker Award as the top college player. They were the first pro-style coaches Eichel had. They knew he was talented, but they also knew once you get to a certain level, almost everyone is talented. What separates those who are good and those who make it all the way to the NHL is find-ing a way to be superior when there's no advantage.

"He was always a top player for his birth year in our area and in the state and New England," said Chris Masters. "The same things that make him special and what I bill a dominant player at the NHL level are a lot of the same things we saw at the midget level for us. He had a long, graceful stride. He had great speed and was deceptive with his speed. But back then he was tall, but he was also skinny and thin, so he didn't have a lot of meat on his bones. I don't care how skilled you are, there's going to be an adjustment period when you're playing against good players who are three or four years older than you. But again, I just think it speaks to how competitive Jack is, how smart he is as a player and he was patient with his development."

Bob Eichel always set his expectations low. He believed his son was good, but he guarded against hype. Part of him wanted Jack to never get a big ego or become full of himself. The other part was he just didn't know any kids who had gone to the NHL and had nothing to compare Jack to. Chris Masters was a little dif-ferent. The first time he saw Eichel play, he wasn't the best or most dominant player. But on every successive viewing, he was better and better. Unlike McDavid, there was a workmanlike quality to him. He was bullish on the ice. He skated with a singular purpose, as though he had been programmed to hunt the puck. Aside from Eichel's speed, shot and overall skills, Masters saw intelligence. Eichel was a real-time problem solver.

He just needed a problem to solve. "Above everything else, what I thought really differentiated Jack from his peers and really elevated his play and the play of his teammates was just how smart he was," said Masters. "He just thought the game better than everybody else. His compete level was off the charts, so when you balance that high compete level with someone who is gifted physically and thinks the game so well, it makes for a special player."

Watching Eichel those first few weeks, however, was like watching someone breaking off the tips of a pencil on the *New York Times* crossword puzzle. Playing with kids who were older meant that he was no longer the fastest or the strongest. For the first time in his career, he wasn't the best player on the ice. "He was a kid," said Masters. "There wasn't a hair on his face and there were pimples coming in. As talented as he was, he was a third-line winger. He didn't complain, he didn't bitch, his parents didn't say a word to us. And Jack trusted that I was the coach and whatever the team wanted me to do, I would do. He was there to learn and work hard and get what he would earn."

Eichel had been used to coming home after a weekend tournament with a dozen goals to his name and an MVP award. Now, as a depth forward, he wasn't even picking up assists. "I definitely struggled," said Eichel. "I don't think I scored a goal until November." After a game in which his son barely touched the puck, Eichel's dad asked Masters if maybe they'd made a mistake. "Don't worry, Bob," said Masters. "He's doing fine. Just be patient."

Eichel and his dad were not the only ones being told to be patient. The other players on the Junior Bruins had been told that this thirteen-year-old kid was special. "It was pretty crazy, because it was the first time a lot of us were playing with a kid that young," said Brendan Leahy, one of Eichel's teammates. "We didn't really know him, because he was so young, but I remember Chris Masters coming up to me and saying, 'Watch out for this kid.'"

Eventually, Eichel caught up. He learned how to find holes in the defence, how to position himself so he wouldn't get hit. On his birthday, he scored his first goal of the season. With that, the floodgates opened. He finished the season with 15 goals and 36 points in 40 games. "He figured out that at this level against these types of kids who were stronger and maybe a little faster, he just needed to be a little bit smarter," said Masters. "And I think his hockey IQ is what really carries him through the day. No one is smarter than him."

There was growth in other areas as well. The pimply kid with the curly hair was playing against seniors in high school and men who were on their way to college. He had to man up as well. "People were targeting him every single game," said Leahy. "It was just one of those things that he had to deal with. But he was good about it. I saw him grow and get stronger and get tougher. Obviously, he was probably the best player when he was little, but that had to be the first time when he had to deal with constantly being hit and slashed and targeted. It was good to see him react in a positive way. Some guys would put a shell on. But he wasn't afraid."

"Chris protected the shit out of him," said Bob Eichel. "If Chris sensed there was going to be a big brawl, he'd have him off the ice. He was just a really good guy for Jack. A really good role model. We'll always be indebted to the Masters family. To the Eichels, they're number one. They did a great job."

The following year, Eichel returned to the Bruins bigger and stronger and a year older. It was almost unfair. He had already figured out how to contribute at 5-foot-9 and 145 pounds. Now, he was two inches taller and about thirty pounds heavier. "That's where it took off," he said. Eichel scored 39 goals and 86 points in 36 games. The Bruins won a national championship. The following year, he went to the USA Hockey National Team Development Program (NTDP) in Ann Arbor, Michigan. He was now playing against the best kids in the country. But he was also playing against his own age group. Again, it was almost unfair.

"He was playing for the Junior Bruins, which I think was an advantage, to be honest," said Bob Eichel. "He was playing against guys who were in high school hockey and the other kids around here were playing against kids their own age. When he went to the [NTDP] tryout, guys didn't push him around. I remember a kid telling [Jack] that [his team] won the U-14 national title and Jack's like, 'We won the Junior B national title.'"

THE BEANPOT IS A HOCKEY TOURNAMENT FEATURING THE FOUR MAJOR college schools in the Boston area—Boston College, Boston University, Harvard University and Northeastern University—that has been held annually since 1952. For some, it's bigger than winning the national title—or even the Stanley Cup.

"That's why you go to college in Boston," said Bob Eichel, who has never missed a Beanpot in more than twenty-five years. "Guys from other places don't get it. They don't understand. But around here, it's all that matters.

"I'll tell you one quick story here. Jack Parker, the former Boston University head coach who I consider the greatest coach going, told me one time that he won a national title and he was at an event in the summer and a guy walked up to him and said, 'How did you do this year?' And Jack goes, 'We won a national title.' The guy looks at him like he's unimpressed. 'Well... how did you do in the Beanpot?' That's all that matters to people around here."

BOB EICHEL CRIED THAT DAY. HE DIDN'T CRY WHEN HIS SON was drafted into the NHL, but he cried when Jack announced he was going to college. His mom cried too. Everyone did. By then, it was obvious that Jack was going to play Division-1 in the NCAA. Pretty much every school in the country had been offering him a full scholarship since he had led the Junior Bruins to a national title at fourteen years old. The only question was which one he was going to pick. In the end, it came down to two choices: Boston College and Boston University (BU).

Each one held significance. His father's team was Boston University, maybe more so than the Bruins. Growing up, it had been Bob Eichel's dream to play for the Terriers. Where he came from, that meant you had made it. Boston University is where Keith Tkachuk, Chris Drury and so many players from the 1980 "Miracle on Ice" Olympic team, including Jack O'Callahan, Jim Craig and Mike Eruzione, had all played. It was where the legendary Jack Parker, "the greatest coach going," was working the final few seasons of a forty-year career.

"[Boston University] is the dream," said Bob Eichel. "At one point, it was more than playing in the NHL. Guys I knew played at BU. A lot of guys I grew up with and went to school with. Growing up, you had the Bruins and Bobby Orr and you had BU hockey. I mean, [BU] was the thing when I was a little kid. I only went to see the Bruins play once in my life. But you could afford to see BU play."

Jack, however, had always been a Boston College fan. He didn't know why, exactly. Maybe it was because the Masters brothers both went there. Maybe it was to add a little spice to a father-son rivalry, something he and his dad could razz each other over. "We'd go at it when they played each other," said Jack. "He would root for BU and I'd root for BC."

"We'd sit there and watch and go back and forth, and back and forth," said Bob Eichel, laughing. "It was a rivalry."

For a while, it looked like Eichel was going to choose Boston College. His school. His choice. But then one day he came home and handed his dad a Boston University hat and his mom a Boston University sweatshirt. Just like that, with a big Cheshire-cat grin spread across his face. The place flooded with tears. "When he went to BU it was probably the happiest day of my life," said Bob Eichel. "I was shocked. We all were shocked. Everybody was shocked."

"I think he started crying," said Jack Eichel. "He and my mom both started crying. My sister was there. It was a nice situation, a nice little moment." There were reasons that went beyond making his mom and dad happy for choosing Boston University. It was a city school and Jack was a city kid. He felt more at home on a campus right next to Fenway Park, rather than the suburbs.

"The hockey players are for the most part from a more working-class area in Boston," said Eichel, "where more of the wealthier kids go to BC. Don't get me wrong, I had a lot of friends who went to BC who aren't wealthy kids. I thought that the kids and the situation and the environment was just better for me at BU. It ended up being a better fit."

In some ways, playing at Boston University was the pinnacle of everything that Eichel had worked for. In his parents' eyes, he had made it. They never really talked about the NHL around the house. "[BU] was kind of my parents' biggest goal," said Jack. "When I was young, my parents were like, 'I hope you can make the high school varsity team.' And then when I did that, they're like, 'I hope you can go to college. Imagine if you could get a scholarship playing hockey? Imagine if you could go to Boston University?' It just keeps growing."

Eichel spent only one year at Boston University before he was drafted into the NHL and began his pro career. But he crammed a lot into that one year. He won the Hobey Baker Award and led the Terriers to the national title. In the process, he got his first taste of what stardom truly looks like.

Stardom was startling, not only to Jack but to his father as well. "I remember calling him, saying, 'Jesus, how are the practices going? Are you going to be able to play third line, get ten to twelve minutes a game?'" Eichel told him that he was on the first line. "And he was like, 'You can't be on friggin' first line at BU, this is BU you're talking about.' It was friggin' unbelievable."

BU coach David Quinn laughed at that story. It shows just how humble the family was. They knew Eichel was a great player and everything, but they respected the process. They expected that as a freshman he would have to earn his dues, work his way up the lineup. It was the same way when he was drafted by the Buffalo Sabres and refused his favourite number because he hadn't yet made the team. "But I'm no dummy," said Quinn. "I'm not putting Jack Eichel on the fourth line. I don't care how old he is."

Eichel was a star on campus. The students all knew him. They cheered for him. They followed him around—even to away games. Indeed, the Terriers needed Eichel to be the star. And he didn't disappoint. "It was his very first game. We were in UMass Amherst and we were up 2–1 after the second period and he hadn't had a point yet, and five minutes later he had three points and the game was 5–1," said Quinn. "He changed the whole complexion of the game."

It was like that all year. Eichel finished with 26 goals and 71 points in 40 games and was named the top player in the country—only the second freshman since Paul Kariya to do so. Boston University was dominant all year long, but ended up losing in the NCAA championship final 4–3 to Providence on a fluky shot that bounced in off goalie Matt O'Connor. "It was a magical year for him—for us, for me," said Quinn. "Obviously losing in the national championship the way we did was devastating, but he won the Hobey Baker, led the country in scoring, and we had a great team. For Jack it was time to go."

"Now that I've had time to reflect on what I did, it's quite incredible how much our team accomplished," said Eichel. "It was a great year. I think all the goals I had were met or almost met." At least they were for Eichel's dad. After all, Boston University had won the Beanpot.

NO QUESTION, THE BUFFALO Sabres wanted to pick first overall. They wanted McDavid. In 2014–15, they did everything they could to make it happen, including holding a fire sale that saw the team trade away three goalies and win just 23 of 82 games. It was a tank job like no other. Fans, who started showing up to the rink in "McDavid" jerseys,

I feel for the fans. I mean, we went through a tough year and I think that they were extremely excited about Connor. If you can pick one or two, you're going to choose one... any time you can get one vs. two in any walk of life, you're going to want number one.

— **TIM MURRAY, former Buffalo Sabres general manager, on the night of the NHL Draft Lottery**

began booing when the Sabres scored in close games and cheering whenever a goal went in on their goalie. It was embarrassing. But with a once-in-a-generation player waiting for whoever picked first, it was the reality of the situation.

Of course, finishing in last place overall didn't guarantee that Buffalo would get the No. 1 pick. A draft lottery had been implemented years earlier to dissuade teams from purposely losing. So when the Edmonton Oilers ended up winning the lottery and picked first, you could almost see the hockey gods having a good laugh.

Eichel knew he wasn't Buffalo's first choice. But he also knew that minds could change. Although he would never admit it, he liked having a rival to push him to be better. He needed McDavid in the same way that Batman needed the Joker or Superman needed Lex Luthor.

"I'm not competing with Connor," Eichel told *Sports Illustrated* in 2015. And yet they did compete against each other. And when they did, people took notice. "At the U-17 tournament in Canada, [Jack] played against Connor McDavid and Ekblad and all the guys with Team Ontario," said Bob Eichel. "He had a really good game. And a friend of mine and I drove up there in a snowstorm and watched it—it took us like nine hours to drive it—and I looked at my buddy and he said, 'Now do you think he's going to play in the NHL?' 'Yeah, I think he's got a chance.'"

At the U-18 world championship in Sochi, Russia, the United States lost to Canada in the gold medal final. McDavid was the tournament MVP, scoring 8 goals and 14 points in 7 games. After the tournament, Eichel returned home and trained harder and harder. He enlisted the help of Kim Brandvold, a skating coach, and hit the gym even harder. When McDavid led the Oilers to the playoffs—and won the scoring title and league MVP—and Eichel's Sabres missed the playoffs once again, he went back home that summer and trained even harder.

If a picture of McDavid wasn't on the back of Eichel's bedroom door, it seemed to be plastered on his mind. "I would definitely say he was driven and motivated by [Connor]," said Ferri. "Being his closest friend, I'd always ask him, 'Do you think you're better than him?' He never really said yes or no, he just said it made him work harder in the gym. McDavid was probably doing the same thing. You just use it as a motivation kind of thing."

Eichel looks at it differently. McDavid isn't the reason why he works harder. It doesn't matter who's on his bedroom door— Eichel is still going to try to get better. He's a worker, he says. Always has been. It's what his parents are and what defines him as a native of North Chelmsford. "I just feel good about myself after I work," said Eichel. "You want to get better, right? You want to be the best. The only way to get better is to work. That's always been my motto."

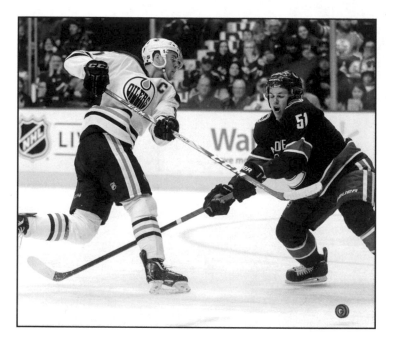

EDMONTON OILERS
» № 97 «

POSITION	CENTRE
SHOOTS	LEFT
HEIGHT	6'1"
WEIGHT	192 LB
BORN	JANUARY 13, 1997
BIRTHPLACE	RICHMOND HILL, ON, CAN
DRAFT	2015 EDM, 1ST RD, 1ST PK (1ST OVERALL)

Connor McDavid takes a shot on net in a 2018 game against the Vancouver Canucks. The Canadian Press/Darryl Dyck

Connor McDavid

THERE HAVE BEEN COUNTLESS STORIES WRITTEN AND retold about Connor McDavid, the wunderkind Wayne Gretzky said was the best nineteen-year-old he had ever seen and who Sidney Crosby said "reminded me of myself" as a kid.

Sherry Bassin could tell you a hundred of them alone. His favourite is when, as Erie Otters' general manager, he drove four hours from, Erie, Pennsylvania, to Newmarket, Ontario, to take McDavid out for lunch, only to find out that the teenager had forgot all about him and stood him up. At least, that's what Bassin thought at the time. The way he tells it, it had been a hot and humid summer day in July—"twenty-eight or thirty degrees"— and Bassin was supposed to pick up McDavid from his parents' house after a morning workout. Except Bassin couldn't find him.

He rang the doorbell. Nothing. He called McDavid's cellphone. It went to voicemail. He looked in the driveway. A car was parked there, but no one was inside. *What's going on?* Bassin thought. Eventually he said to hell with it and started to walk away.

"And that's when the garage door went up," said the seventy-seven-year-old in a voice that's become permanently hoarse from a lifetime of shouting in cold hockey arenas. "Mac's in there on rollerblades shooting pucks and he's got it all set up with obstacles and stuff. This is in the afternoon! And he's soaked! And had blisters on his hands and stuff."

"Give me ten more minutes," said an out-of-breath McDavid, barely stopping to greet Bassin. "And I remember he says to me, 'The shot's got to get better, Bass. It's got to get better.' The kid had scored 120 points in 47 games that year!"

Some things never change. Fast-forward a couple of years and the twenty-year-old Edmonton Oilers captain has just wrapped up his second season in the NHL and is now sitting in a luxurious suite inside the Wynn Las Vegas. It's the morning of the NHL Awards and in a few hours McDavid will have a night for the ages. In addition to being awarded the Art Ross Trophy for leading the league in overall scoring with 100 points, he will also be voted as the winner of the Hart Memorial Trophy and Ted Lindsay Award as the league's most valuable player as judged by reporters covering the game and the NHL Players' Association, respectively.

He is literally the best player in the NHL and the face of a future generation of star players, something EA Sports recognized by splashing his picture on the cover of its latest NHL 18 video game. And yet, sitting on a white couch in a plain white T-shirt and denim shorts, he still sounds like a kid who wants the garage door closed so he can continue working on his perceived deficiencies.

"I think I want to get a better shot and want to be more dangerous from the outside, definitely from that half-wall position on the power play," said McDavid, who in 2017–18 won a second straight Art Ross Trophy and Ted Lindsay Award after finishing with a league-best 108 points. "You have to be able to shoot and score out there. It's definitely something I'm going to work on."

True to his word, shortly after returning from Vegas, McDavid was firing pucks back inside the sauna that his mom calls his "shooting range." It is here, inside a two-car garage with holes in the drywall and puck marks on the plywood his father installed to cover up the holes, where McDavid spent most of his time growing up. It's here where he and his older brother created what Connor called the "most ridiculous" obstacle course out of empty paint cans, skateboards and extra hockey sticks; where he shot his daily chore of one hundred pucks; where he learned how to take a corner like a Formula One race car; and where he became a player who can stickhandle and skate with the puck faster than most players skate without it. Garage door closed, it became his sanctuary.

"For me, it's soothing when you're out there," said McDavid. "You put your phone away and put some music on and you just get away from it all. I just enjoy that. I like doing it now more than I did before. Back then, it wasn't a lot of fun. You were out there because you needed to get better. You thought if you did that, you would go places."

"Generational" players are obviously born with a lot of natural talent, but they are not necessarily born with greatness. That takes work, dedication and shooting puck after puck after puck. You look at McDavid today and just see a kid who has an effortless stride and an ability to think the game at a microcomputer speed, like he's not even trying. You don't see what he was doing behind closed doors throughout his youth. And what he is still doing now to become even better.

"I know when one of the guys was picking Connor up for the pro camp in the summer in Toronto, he said they were almost late getting here because he couldn't find him," said Joe Quinn, McDavid's long-time personal skills coach. "And sure enough, he was in the garage. It was one hundred degrees outside and he's in the garage ripping around in his rollerblades right before the pro skate. I kind of laughed at that."

HE WOULD COME TO ME SOME DAYS AND SAY, "MOM, I'M REALLY TIRED. I just don't want to shoot pucks."

I would say, "Okay, don't shoot pucks."

Then he'd say, "But I'll be really upset with myself if I don't."

And I'd say, "Okay, go shoot pucks then. But you also have to listen to your body. If you're tired, listen to your body."

But he would say, "No, I'd feel really bad."

Even now, he still shoots pucks.

KELLY McDAVID'S YOUNGEST SON WAS DIFFERENT. EVEN when he was young, she knew that much. Cameron was the laid-back older brother, the one who rolled with the punches and navigated life without a road map or compass. At four years younger, Connor was wound noticeably tighter. He was the kind of kid who needed constant stimulus, the reason why fidget spinners were invented.

"Every day it was, 'What are we doing?' What are we doing at this time, what are we doing at that time?' A few weeks into summer, he'd be a little crazy," said Kelly. "I'd be like, 'Oooohkay, we're just going to hang out today?' Where Cameron would hang out every day. He would be thrilled by that."

Kelly was the one who Connor would drag down into the family's then-unfinished basement and force into playing goaltender as he worked on his shot. He'd ask his grandmother to play in net if his mom was busy. "And then when he started to be able to lift it up, that was it," said Kelly. "We were like, 'No way.'"

That didn't stop Connor. Grabbing as many stuffed animals as he could hold, he arranged his "fans" along the basement walls and pretended he was playing in the NHL. "Mom!" he would yell from the basement. "I just won the Stanley Cup!"

If he wasn't playing hockey, then he was watching it, either on TV or tagging along to his older brother's practices and games. When Cameron began playing competitively with the Newmarket Redmen and had to wear a dress shirt and tie to games, Connor did the same. A friend of the family even gave him a used team jacket and matching hat to complete the outfit.

"He would go into the dressing room for the pre-game talk, because they sort of made him the trainer's helper," said Kelly. "When you'd talk to the coach afterward, he'd say the only person really listening was Connor. He was a sponge. When he watched hockey, he was glued to the TV. You could tell he was absorbing everything. He could watch a game and he could pick things out. He had really good hockey sense."

This hockey sense is what carried McDavid through his early days. He was always a good skater, balanced and confident on his two feet, but the thing his parents noticed was how he read the game. When kids are starting out in hockey, they don't stick to their position because they don't know what that means. Instead, they move in one large pack toward the puck and fight over it like they are in the middle of a rugby scrum. McDavid was smarter than that. Without being told, he stood just outside the pack and waited for the puck to come loose. He'd then skate up the ice with it and score. "And then the parents would have a fit because then he was a puck hog," said Kelly, laughing.

Soon, he was putting up ridiculous numbers. Even older kids started to notice. "He played in the early afternoon and we'd play at night," said Cameron. "And some guys on my team would watch him play and say, 'Man, your brother's insane!' I would be like, 'Yeah, I guess.' 'No, he's going to be in the NHL, for sure.'"

McDavid was so good that playing recreational house league hockey against kids his own age was not benefiting him or the other kids, who were standing around and watching as this six-year-old scored goals at will. The problem was the Newmarket Minor Hockey Association did not allow six-year-olds to play competitive rep hockey until they turned seven, with no exceptions.

"Brian [Connor's dad] really tried to argue the point that when kids are good at school they skip a grade," said Kelly. "But they said no." So McDavid went to Aurora, where the administrators could see that this was a special circumstance—so special that they moved him all the way up to play with nine-year-olds. He dominated, but it was a difficult year for him. It was still house league hockey, where the competition wasn't great and the games weren't taken seriously.

One day, Kelly's youngest son said that he didn't want to play house league anymore. It wasn't fun. He only wanted to play rep. She told him to be patient and he'd get his chance to play rep next season. But to Connor, even a few months of waiting was an eternity. So she came up with a solution. Grabbing a pen and a sheet of paper, she drew a picture of a stairwell. On each step she wrote the date of his upcoming games. On the very top step, she wrote, TRYOUTS.

"Every time a game was over, he would come home and cross it off," she said. "With him, I realized you had to break things down in smaller pieces because he sees this big goal and will get frustrated because it's not happening fast enough or he's not getting there fast enough.

"Even when he broke his collarbone a couple of years ago, he was devastated obviously. But when we talked to the doctors, we said that you have to give him things to expect at certain times. You have to tell him that in two weeks he'll be able to do this and in four weeks he'll be able to do that. You have to give him milestones to achieve. You can't tell him that in three months he'll be healed, because that just won't fly with him. So when he had those little milestones and he was hitting those milestones before they said he probably would, he was feeling even better. He had control over it."

McDavid craves control and finds comfort in routines and the feeling that something is being done with a purpose in mind. It is why he didn't just shoot pucks every day but took at least one hundred shots, because that was the number his father came up with as a baseline for achieving greatness and reaching the NHL. Each day, each shot, was a step in the process.

Sometimes the routines would become silly. On the way to games, his dad always popped in the same mix CD in the car stereo. Track one was "All Along the Watchtower" by Jimi Hendrix, followed by Soundgarden's "Black Hole Sun."

"A bunch of random songs, honestly, songs that I would never listen to today," said McDavid. "They were definitely songs my dad liked. He put together the CD." Others might have gotten sick of listening to the same songs over and over again. Not McDavid. Part of him believed the music prepared him for the game, was somehow the reason why he was so effective on the ice. "[The CD] got worn out and they had to re-burn it with all the same songs," said Cameron. "They listened to it once before a game, so then we had to listen to it every time after. I'm sure my dad was super excited that he got to listen to his tunes. Connor had all these weird superstitions."

"Some call it superstition, some call it routine," said McDavid. "I don't know, I think it had a little bit of both in the end. For me, a lot of it was routine. I think it's important for athletes to have a certain routine and have things that you think will help you perform better. If it works, it works."

When does routine turn into superstition? McDavid isn't sure, but it's probably when a twelve-year-old son gets to sit shotgun on the way to the rink—pushing his mom to the back seat—because the last time he sat up front the team won and he had played a great game. "My mom thought it was ridiculous that she was in the back and her twelve-year-old son was in the front," said Cameron, laughing.

It was the side effect of having a son who took the sport seriously. Maybe a little too seriously. "If he lost, it would just be the end of the world," said his mom. "When he was little he would cry and as he got older he would get mad. Cameron and I used to joke that if they lost a game, he and I should just stay in a hotel because they're going to be miserable when they get home."

"If they lost, it was just brutal," said Cameron. "It would be quiet at the dinner table and nobody would say much. He was like that with everything. When he and I used to play card games or board games as kids, if he wasn't going to win he would say, 'I'm not going to play anymore.' And it was frustrating as a brother. You have this buddy that you want to play with all the time, but he's just too afraid to lose."

Connor McDavid plays for the York Simcoe Express. Photo courtesy of the McDavid family

Luckily for Connor's brother and mom, there wasn't much losing to go around when Connor was growing up. Once he started playing Triple-A, for the York Simcoe Express, the team was stacked. Sam Bennett, who was selected fourth overall by the Calgary Flames in the 2014 NHL Entry Draft, was a long-time teammate. So was defenceman Travis Dermott, a second-round pick of the Toronto Maple Leafs, and several other players who would go on to play college or university hockey.

But even on a star-studded roster, McDavid stood out. He was the kid who could slow down the pace of the game or ramp it up to his level, the one who wouldn't score until he had literally skated around the opposing team—sometimes twice.

Jack Doak, the team's assistant coach, noticed that it wouldn't take long for spectators to realize that one kid was considerably better than the others. "His hockey IQ was off the charts from a very young age. He was like a pro hockey player when he was eight years old. His demeanour coming into the rink, his demeanour getting ready for a game, how he conducted himself in workouts, how he conducted himself in practices, the kid was just always on. The kid approached things very seriously and with purpose."

"I remember before every practice and every game, he'd be stickhandling with his dad in the hallway," said Dermott. "It was unheard of."

The Express were practically unbeatable during McDavid's time on the team. They won five OMHA titles and four straight provincial championships. When they did lose, McDavid took it personally. "In minor atom, we lost one game to the Whitby Wildcats during the regular season and we ended up playing against them in the final of the OMHA championship," said Doak, whose son Aidan was York Simcoe's goalie. "Mitch Marner was on [the Wildcats] and I will tell you that Connor was hell-bent that we weren't going to get beat by the Wildcats again."

With the score tied 0–0 in the final, Marner took a penalty in the second period. Once it expired, he popped out of the penalty box and picked up a loose puck for a breakaway. Aidan Doak made the save. What happened next was a move that has become typical of McDavid. Grabbing the puck below the goal line, he took off, sprinting the entire distance of the ice before deking past a stunned goaltender for the game-winning goal.

"It wasn't like he was just one of the guys," said Aidan Doak. "If Connor was coming down on you, you never knew what he was going to do. He scored a beautiful goal. We ended up winning 1–0 and Whitby hadn't lost a game all year long. The next year we went undefeated and swept the whole OMHA."

IF YOU WANT TO KNOW HOW McDAVID BECAME ONE OF THE fastest players in the NHL, don't watch him on an ice surface that is two hundred feet long and eighty-five feet wide. Instead, shrink it down and take a tour of his parents' two-car garage—what Kelly McDavid calls "the disaster zone."

She says this with a hint of pride. After all, each hole in the drywall, each puck mark, is a reminder of how much work her youngest son put in to achieve his dream. "It used to bother me a little bit, because I'd be in the kitchen and there would be all this banging going on," said Kelly McDavid. "Bang! It would hit the door. Bang! It would hit the wall. And I'd be a little worried, like the boys are destroying the house. But Brian was happy about it. 'Shoot away,' he'd say."

It was Brian's idea that Cameron and Connor take one hundred shots each and every day. Not 50. One hundred. Every day. No days off. He said it would make them great, putting it in their heads that it was their path to the NHL. "Brian would say you have to shoot one hundred pucks a day," said Kelly. "And if you don't shoot one hundred pucks a day, it's up to you. But if you want to be successful, this is sort of what you have to do."

"We took that pretty seriously," said Cameron. "Connor more so, obviously."

Brian McDavid, who coached both of his sons, is a big proponent of the 100 per cent rule when it comes to effort. "There's no substitute for hard work," he said. If you wanted to be successful at something, you had to dedicate yourself to it. All the time. No exceptions.

> Small areas are the name of the game. It's all about overloading your motor skills, by stickhandling and skating on your edges. Small touches. Most guys can't do it. They just can't. With Connor, everything is so synchronized. All his motor skills work so fluidly together, so when he cuts left or cuts right, he doesn't have any drag and he's not losing any speed—he's actually getting faster. He can handle the puck at high speeds because he's been doing it his whole life.
>
> **— JOE QUINN, skills coach, Power Edge Pro**

"That's something that I say too," said Cameron, an accomplished musician who became an investment banker at UPS. "Once I decided that I wasn't going to pursue hockey and I went to school, I didn't do that well and then I sort of applied his philosophy and worked as hard as I could in this business program I was in. I'd go to the library every day for hours and study my ass off. The hockey training is definitely applicable."

Whereas Cameron's brother applied it to hockey. Connor was in the garage every day taking his one hundred shots. It was more work than fun. A hundred of anything is a lot. You get past the twenty-five-shot mark and you're still feeling good. Once you pass the halfway mark, you start feeling it in your hand and wrist. At seventy-five, it becomes a mental and physical grind. You want to get to the end so badly that you stop concentrating, start flubbing the puck. By the time you get to one hundred, you just want to drop your stick and go do something else.

Connor McDavid (left) and his brother Cameron receive hockey-themed gifts on Christmas morning. Both boys were crazy about hockey and shot a hundred pucks a day in their garage. Photo courtesy of the McDavid family

"I'd go out there with him and we'd both be doing the drills," said Cameron. "I think I'd give it an hour, an hour and a bit. He'd stay out for two or more."

Whereas Cameron couldn't wait until it was over, Connor loved the rhythmic motion of shooting pucks. He went into a zone, hearing nothing but the sound of the stick scraping against the cement followed by the swish of the puck getting caught in the netting. Even the misses held an appeal—thanks to a father who rewarded the boys for their ability to shoot so hard that pucks went through the drywall. That's how the challenge started.

"My dad went to Home Depot and bought these really thick plywood boards and said, 'All right, if you guys can put it through this, I'll call the NHL scouts,'" said Cameron. "Sure enough, a couple of months later, one of us put a puck through and we went running to our dad like, 'Dad, come see!'"

At first, the boys were in their running shoes when they fired their one hundred pucks. Then they strapped on their roller-blades to make it feel closer to actual hockey. They hung targets. They came up with competitions, like who could hit the most posts, or played games of "horse" like other kids. Then they got really creative.

It started with a couple of leftover paint cans, which the boys set down like pylons that had to be weaved through before shoot-ing. Slowly, they started adding more obstacles. A skateboard that you had to put the puck underneath, a stick resting on two more paint cans that you had to hop over, a shoe you had to wheel around. It kept evolving. "At one point, we decided to take it out of the garage and take over the whole driveway."

"It was a different way to train," said McDavid. "I was always a little inventive. I was always trying to be on my skates as much as possible. You're in the garage and you're trying to do things, but it's very small, so you create obstacles. It was a tight space. That's how hockey is today. It's tight spaces."

Said Cameron, "It was really the most ridiculous thing ever."

For neighbours, it was also ridiculous. The McDavids became that family with the two crazy kids who were out on their driveway every day, jumping over hockey sticks and deking around paint cans. Even when the garage door was closed, the sound of pucks hitting posts or plywood echoed down the quiet street. The intensity with which McDavid went through the drills—along with the "goalie graveyard" of broken nets resting against the side of the house—gave the impression that he was being coached into training like this.

"I saw him every day when I was coming home from work," said Martin Harding, whose son is a friend of McDavid. "He'd be playing in the driveway and I'd come inside and see my kid and he was playing Xbox. I'd be like, 'Do you see what Connor's doing out there?' My kid did his fair share of playing hockey, but Connor was ridiculous. He was in the driveway jumping over paint cans, honing his craft. And he loved it. It wasn't like his dad was out there cracking the whip."

"As time went on, once he got into peewee or bantam, you'd hear people say, 'Oh, his dad's pushing him. Brian's making him do this, Brian's making him do that,'" said Jack Doak. "But you know what, the exact opposite was true. For both Brian and Kelly, they were both trying to keep him grounded and maybe trying to pull him in from the garage. They weren't forcing him to do anything. The kid just ate it up."

When McDavid began to train with skating coach Joe Quinn a few years later, the driveway obstacle course didn't seem so ridiculous.

Quinn, who is the creator of Power Edge Pro, littered the ice with spare tires, auditorium chairs and long four-by-fours with notches so that pucks could slide through them. With the exceptions of a couple of paint cans and a skateboard, it was pretty much what McDavid had been doing all along.

"It was a little bit of a variation of what I was doing," said McDavid. "You don't know what you're doing is going to make you accomplish something one day, you're just having fun training."

"Our stories are very similar," said Joe Quinn. "Obviously I was put on the path to meet Connor. He was already doing the paint cans and stuff like that in the garage. And I started the same way Connor did, in small areas, but with chairs and wood and tires and anything else I could find."

Training in a small area, said Quinn, is the key to what allows McDavid to play at a pace previously unseen in the NHL. Aside from a breakaway, there isn't a whole lot of sprinting up the ice with the puck. Players take quick bursts of speed, manoeuvring in and out of traffic, executing tight turns, evading bodies and sticks, stopping and starting, cutting left and right. And you're doing all this while stickhandling and keeping your head on a swivel. It's like a juggler on a unicycle or playing the drums while singing. You're constantly multi-tasking, asking your hands and feet to work in sync. That takes muscle memory and it takes years and years of practice—the kind of practice McDavid was doing every day inside his garage and out on his driveway, where there wasn't a lot of space.

"You think about it now and it's genius," said Harding. "He's doing all that in a double-car driveway, where he's running out onto the grass if he can't make the turn. It's what everyone wants their kid to do and what they should be doing."

Ask Quinn why McDavid is so fast with the puck and he doesn't mention his edges or balance or coordination. Instead, he talks about his work ethic. Learning how to play at a fast pace does not come naturally to anyone. It's teaching your mind and body to do things that they inherently don't want to do. It's not a fun way to spend the day.

Even with his base training of stickhandling on his driveway, McDavid was still five years younger than the other players Quinn was teaching, many of whom were elite hockey players who had been drafted in the first round and were on their way to an NHL career. At first, he wasn't the best. Not even close. But he was the most determined.

"I always tell this particular story of this one drill that we call 'edge control,'" said Quinn. "You're going over an apparatus that is six inches high and we want [you] to land on the inside edge of your back foot. People who watch it are blown away.

"Well, he's not getting it because the co-ordination it takes to go from [his] strong side to his weak side is unnatural and he's not landing on his inside edge perfectly. No one's getting it. And everyone else wanted to move on and go scrimmage, but he said no, he wants to keep at it because he hasn't mastered it."

This isn't a story of how McDavid mastered the technique later that day. Or later that month. "We did this drill for three years," said Quinn. "These were difficult repetitions and we gradually increased higher levels of difficulty because when you overload most players can't do it." Think about that for a second: McDavid practising a drill for three years, pretty much failing every time, until he finally mastered it. By then, he could have got his PhD in edge control, except he was on to the next challenge.

"I remember Connor saying to me after a game, 'I feel I have so much space when I come out of the wall in the cycle,'" said Quinn. "He feels like he has so much room because he's been practising in what feels like high traffic."

JEFF JACKSON'S PHONE RANG AND SAM GAGNER WAS ON THE OTHER END. Gagner, an NHL forward, had just come back from a summer skate in Toronto and couldn't believe what he had seen. There was this kid on the ice. He couldn't have been more than twelve years old, but he didn't play like any twelve-year-old. "You have to find this kid," Gagner told Jackson, an NHL player agent. "He's doing stuff that I can't even do and I've been in the NHL for five years."

"What's his name?" asked Jackson.

"I think his name is David O'Connor. I know he plays for the Marlboros."

So Jackson called the Toronto Marlboros and said, "Who's this David O'Connor kid you've got playing there?"

There was laughter on the other end. "You mean Connor McDavid?"

OFTEN, PARENTS CAN BE GUILTY OF THINKING THEIR CHIL-dren are much better than they really are. Their son, the piano player, is going to be the next Mozart. Their daughter is going to the National Ballet. Kelly McDavid is the opposite. Her husband

Connor McDavid plays for the Toronto Marlboros. Photo courtesy of McDavid family

would tell her and everyone else that Connor was not only special enough to make the NHL, but to make it and be a star, and Brian would sound like another proud father pumping up his son.

"I was very careful," she said. "I didn't want to jump too far ahead. You hear these stories about kids who were really good hockey players and how they're going to go to the NHL and then you never hear from them again. I was always, 'Just wait, relax, it's still early.' It wasn't until he was playing for the Toronto Marlboros when I'd see him do things and be like, 'Oh my God, did anyone else see that? That was unbelievable!'"

McDavid, who scored 79 goals and 209 points in 88 games, was named the player of the year in the Greater Toronto Hockey League (GTHL). Still, Kelly McDavid tempered her expectations.

When her son applied for exceptional status in 2012—a year after 6-foot-4 defenceman Ekblad had received approval—so that he could enter the OHL a year early, she wasn't sure he would be accepted. After all, how many exceptions to the rule could there be? "I thought they're not going to give exceptional status two years in a row, because it's exceptional."

Sherry Bassin, however, had no doubt McDavid was ready for the OHL as a fifteen-year-old. "Our scouts came to me and said, 'What do you think?' I don't want to sound demeaning or be disrespectful, but my comment was a blind man could pick him out just by listening to him skate. It was just so obvious." Bassin was so impressed by McDavid that he went back to Erie and started stripping the Otters of anything valuable. He wanted that first pick. "We had a team that was good enough to make the playoffs, but we'd be out in the first round or something," said Bassin. "I wasn't interested in having that. I remember our head coach came up to me and said, 'Well, you don't want to win.'"

"We had a good team the year before and then we got off to a bad start and began shipping guys out," said Greg McKegg, who was traded to London. "It was wholesale. Basically everyone was gone." It worked. The Otters won just ten games that year—nine fewer than the next-best team—and finished dead last. McDavid was theirs. Now they just had to figure out how to use him properly.

It was a learning process, both for the team and the player. At first, they sheltered him. A 6-foot-3, 215-pound forward named Stephen Harper had been hand-picked by Bassin to play older brother for the fifteen-year-old rookie. They shared a billet family and were linemates in McDavid's OHL debut. "He could have easily had four or five points if I could've put the puck in the net," said Harper.

"It was interesting, because I had him on a line with guys that weren't overly offensive but were physically strong," said Robbie

Ftorek, who coached McDavid for his first year and a half in Erie. "Had he been with some offensive players, he would have had three or four assists on his first night. Connor was already developed past other guys and they weren't expecting him to pass to them when he did. It was a bit humorous and I felt bad for Connor not getting what he deserved, but that was part of the deal."

McDavid eventually started to pick up points, finishing with 66 points in 63 games as a sixteen-year-old. But those were lean days. The losses started to pile up again for the Otters, who missed the playoffs. "I remember that year was ridiculous," said forward Connor Brown. "We lost like thirty-five games by one goal or something. We weren't getting blown out like the year before. They were close games. And then the switch flipped when we had fifty-three wins a year later."

For McDavid, the losing was something new to adjust to. He had practically never lost while playing for the York Simcoe Express and the Toronto Marlboros. And now he was losing just about every other night. As the first overall pick, a player everyone expected to come in and be a saviour, he took it personally.

"It was early November and we got beaten something like 5–3 on an empty-netter," said Bassin. "He had two or three breakaways and hit the post once and missed on another. I happened to be walking out to the bus, just me and him, and he apologized sincerely, said, 'Mr. Bassin, I'm sorry for letting the team down. If I had done my job we would have won the game.' And this was with nobody around. This wasn't something he was trying to make a big show of it. That's the kind of kid he was."

It was around that time that McDavid was starting to lose some of his confidence. During a game that went into an overtime shootout, Ftorek tapped McDavid on the shoulder and said to get ready, he would be going first. "Pick someone else," said McDavid, who didn't think he could win the game.

"Listen to me," said Ftorek. "You're going to be taking shoot-outs for the rest of your life. You will take every shootout and you will not worry about it. Just be yourself."

It was part of the growth process, said Ftorek. For the first time in McDavid's life, he was being challenged. "He ended up taking them and I think he missed his first three," said Ftorek. "But I kept putting him out there because I felt that was something he needed to overcome and be comfortable with. He had such a long range side to side that he could change the angle of the shot very easily. And he needed to develop calmness to deke around the goaltender. I hope he doesn't hold it against me. But for his development, I felt that I needed to do that for him."

There were other things McDavid learned while in Erie. With every game that passed, his popularity grew. As well, the target on his back got so big that it could be seen across the country. Teams slashed and hacked and tried to get him off his game, knowing that McDavid was a huge part of the team's success. Usually, there was a teammate who took care of things for him. But during a game against the Mississauga Steelheads in November 2014, McDavid had enough and fought Bryson Cianfrone. In the process, he broke his hand with an errant punch that hit the lip of the boards. "When I saw him going off the ice holding his hand—even though I had just turned seventy-eight—I felt like I had turned ninety," said Bassin. "I was in the hospital with him and I looked at him and said, 'Mac, why?' And he said, 'I can't have everybody else fighting my battles.'"

McDavid's hand healed in time for the World Junior Championship, where he tied for first in scoring with 11 points in 7 games to help Canada win its first gold medal in six years. He then returned to Erie, where the Otters won their division with 104 points but lost a best-of-seven series 4–1 in the OHL Final to the Oshawa Generals. By then, McDavid mania had reached peak level.

"By the third year, it was pretty crazy. We really couldn't go anywhere," said McDavid's billet host Bob Catalde. "We were getting all sorts of mail. My dining room table was like our holding spot for all the stuff that needed to be signed and read and everything else. It was just piles and piles of stuff."

"You could tell that he was going to turn the franchise around," said Harper. "I think at the time it wasn't a great team or fanbase and didn't have a great reputation for players to go there and stuff. And now you see that Erie's one of the better places to play in the league. I think he definitely changed the whole culture. Connor definitely got us into sellouts every night. We became a hockey hotbed."

ON A HOT AFTERNOON IN AUGUST, BOB CATALDE MADE THE same drive from Erie that Sherry Bassin had made several years earlier. Once again, someone was looking for McDavid. And once again, he was nowhere to be found. Except this time, Catalde knew where to look. "As soon as I pull up to his driveway, what's he doing? He's in his garage firing 150 or 200 pucks. We're supposed to play golf and we're going to be late for our tee time. But he said he wasn't going to leave until he fired all these pucks. This kid is not only gifted, but he works hard too. He doesn't stop."

Mitch MARNER

TORONTO MAPLE LEAFS
» № 16 «

POSITION	CENTRE
SHOOTS	RIGHT
HEIGHT	6'0"
WEIGHT	175 LB
BORN	MAY 5, 1997
BIRTHPLACE	MARKHAM, ON, CAN
DRAFT	2015 TOR, 1ST RD, 4TH PK (4TH OVERALL)

Mitch Marner plays for the Maple Leafs at the 2015 NHL Rookie Tournament. The Canadian Press/Dave Chidley

NORMALLY, BONNIE MARNER HAS JUST ONE TEA before the first intermission. One large tea from Tim Hortons that she purchases right before the start of the game and that she then spends the first period sipping, timing her bathroom break with an official break in the action. As the unofficial videographer of the Marner clan, she never dared to miss even a second of her youngest son's hockey games. But then Mitch Marner made it to the NHL and everything changed.

To be fair, it wasn't Bonnie's fault. On the home opener of the 2016–17 season, the Toronto Maple Leafs were honouring their one-hundredth anniversary with a pre-game celebration that seemed to go on forever. By the time the puck finally dropped, Bonnie was already on her second cup. Understandably, nature called much earlier than usual. "I was dying," said Bonnie. "My teeth were floating in the back of my mouth."

Finally, her husband told her to just go. She was safe, said Paul Marner. The Leafs had just taken a penalty and Mitch wasn't on the penalty kill unit. If Bonnie hurried, she probably wasn't going to miss a thing. And then, as she was drying her hands, she heard it: first came the roar of the crowd, followed by the sound of the goal horn as Marner wristed a shot past Boston Bruins goalie Anton Khudobin at 12:52. On the Sportsnet TV broadcast, the camera panned to Paul as play-by-play announcer Jim Hughson said, "Mom and Dad, Paul and Bonnie, celebrate the first National Hockey League goal for Mitchell Marner."

Except Paul was celebrating by himself. Bonnie, meanwhile, was cursing her bad luck. "In the bathroom they play the game and they mentioned number 16 and I thought, 'Bloody hell!' I quickly ran out of the bathroom and I didn't know where I was. I just had to get out to the ice surface," remembered Bonnie. "I celebrated with the ladies who help you find your seat.

"I said, 'What happened?' She said the rookie just got his first goal. It was a beauty. You missed a good one.' And I'm like, 'I'm his mom' and she didn't believe me. She was really nice. She said, 'Oh, you're not old enough to be his mom.'" It was a familiar comment. If Bonnie Marner didn't look like she could be the mother of a nineteen-year-old, then her nineteen-year-old, who has never had to buy a razor and used to eat peanut butter right out of the jar in hopes of packing on weight, didn't look like he was old enough to be in the NHL. Of course, looks can be deceiving.

Marner has always been one of the best and one of the most talented players on any team he's played for. At the age of four, he was dominating against six-year-olds. He won a Junior A championship against twenty-year-olds when he was fifteen and finished second in OHL scoring when he was seventeen. And yet few players have spent their careers being as second-guessed as Marner.

Oh sure, critics would say, he might be able to score goals and put up points at this level. But there's no way he'll be able to do it at the next level. He's far too small, far too frail. And then Marner would get to the next level and prove everyone wrong. But as soon as it came time for him to jump up to another level, those same questions would persist. "A lot of guys didn't think what he was doing was transferable to the next level," said Leafs scout Lindsay Hofford, who has known Marner since he was seven years old. "I even talked to NHL guys and they said he'd be a great junior player but he wouldn't be an NHL player. But they said the same thing about him at the minor hockey level when he was getting drafted to the OHL."

It was not until his rookie season with the Leafs that Marner put all those questions to rest. Marner might have been the only Toronto player who didn't have to worry about GM Lou Lamoriello's ban on facial hair, but he hardly played like a nineteen-year-old kid. In 77 games he tied for third among rookies in scoring with 19 goals and 61 points and was named to the league's All-Rookie Team. Along with Matthews and Nylander, he was one of the main reasons why Toronto went from finishing with the worst record in 2015–16 to qualifying for the playoffs.

If you had doubts about Marner's size, you didn't anymore. "I heard it all my life growing up," Marner, who led the Leafs with 69 points in 2017–18, said of the question marks surrounding his size. "It definitely got annoying. That talk still hasn't gone away yet, but I think one day it will."

THE FIRST TIME SOMEONE unfairly judged Mitchell Marner because of his size was when Paul Marner was trying to find someone to coach his youngest son. Paul Marner always knew Mitch was special. At age two, Mitch could already perform forward and backward crossovers. He could raise the puck well over the net. By the time he started playing organized hockey in Clarington, Ontario, he was competing in a full-contact league against kids who were as much as two years older. CityTV in Toronto had even featured him as an Athlete of

He always wanted to demonstrate. He wanted to be first. He'd put his arm up. I started doing private lessons with him and his brother. Mitch was just so advanced. His brother would try to keep up with him and he couldn't; he would only get the first two parts of the drill, where Mitch would get six or seven parts of the drill no problem from a very young age. And his brother is four years older. [Mitch's] vision and his mind are top of the charts of anyone in the NHL.

— **ROB DESVEAUX, director and head instructor, 3 Zones Hockey** the Week, with a reporter asking if the blond-haired tyke thought he could score a goal on then–Maple Leafs goalie Curtis Joseph. Without hesitation, Mitch looked at the camera and nodded.

Still, Rob Desveaux wasn't sold. When he got a call from Paul Marner asking to train Mitch at 3 Zones Hockey in Ajax, Ontario, Desveaux practically hung up the phone. "I'm not a babysitter," he said. Mitch was four years old then. And although he wasn't exactly a baby, he was still four or more years younger than the youngest kids at Desveaux's hockey school. But Paul Marner persisted. He'd been certain Desveaux was the right person to coach his son ever since he'd seen a young Tyler Seguin dominate against older competition in a local tournament. "I think the game ended up 11–1 and Tyler had nine points," Paul Marner said of Seguin, the second overall pick in 2010. "And he was playing a year up. I just watched him and went, 'Wow.'"

Seguin was seven years old when he first started working with Desveaux, but Paul Marner did not want to wait that long. For months, he kept bugging Desveaux to take on Mitch. For months, Desveaux kept telling him to wait until Mitch was older and bigger. "I don't take kids that age, because you get a lot of parents who think their kids are superstars," said Desveaux. "He kept bugging me to take his kid and after a couple of months I finally said, 'Okay, bring him.'"

There was, however, one small condition. If little Mitch couldn't hold his own—if he couldn't keep up or if he wasn't mature enough to follow instruction—Desveaux warned Paul that his son would pay for it. "He said, 'Bring Mitch to my school on Monday night and if he embarrasses me, I'll have thirty-five kids on the ice and I'm going to drag you and him to centre ice and you'll have to walk him off the ice in front of all the parents and kids,'" said Paul Marner. "So he goes, 'Do you still want to do it?'"

Paul agreed, even though Mitch had no idea what was taking place. "It's funny, because I drive to the rink and Mitch used to nap on the way because he's a baby," said Paul Marner. "I mean, he's four years old. Anyway, I take him there and carry him into the rink because he's still asleep and get him dressed and walk over to the boards."

Said Desveaux: "I was on the ice and somebody said there's a guy here to talk to you. So I see Paul and I say, 'Where's your kid?' And he reached down and pulled him up. He was so small that I didn't even see him over the boards."

"Rob literally rolled his eyes," said Paul.

The eye-rolling ceased as soon as Mitch started skating. As promised, he didn't embarrass anyone. In the first drill, Desveaux asked the group of kids, who were mostly seven- and eight-year-olds, to perform a power turn around a pylon on their forehand side. Then he told them to switch it up and do it on their backhand side. About half of them messed it up and did it on the wrong side. Not Mitch. He was a natural. Paul added another pylon and told the kids to perform figure eights. Mitch executed the drill as though he had been doing it for years.

Desveaux looked over to Paul, who was still standing by the side of the boards, grinning. "He's in," said Desveaux. "I'll work with him anytime."

Others have needed more convincing. Sitting at the kitchen table in his home in Vaughan, Paul Marner opened up a black IBM laptop. "I'm just going to show you something," he said, typing a few words into YouTube. "I made this for him on his draft night." On the screen popped up a highlight package of Mitch, beginning from the time when he was four years old until he was eighteen.

There's a mite-sized Mitch playing against McDavid. And one of him against Michael Dal Colle and another against Robby Fabbri. There's the CityTV clip of when he was Athlete of the Week, one of Mitch evading a bodycheck and one of him celebrating a goal as if it was scored in Game 7 of the Stanley Cup. "That's him going for a hit," said Paul Marner, laughing. "That used to be a big part of his game."

Most of the footage is from Bonnie Marner, his mom, who recorded nearly every second of Mitch's hockey career. Part of the reason she did it was because Mitch wanted to watch his many goals—and dissect his play—immediately after the family came home from a game. The other reason was Paul and Bonnie got tired of all the negative comments the other parents were saying about their youngest son: how he was a puck hog who never passed, how he was too small to ever amount to anything, how they were wasting their time.

Mitch Marner plays for the Vaughan Kings.

Photo courtesy of the Marner family

"After that, they never wanted to come near me," Bonnie Marner said of filming the other parents. "They would say, 'Is that on?' I'd say, 'Yeah, I'm catching every word you say.' It would get people so mad."

Paul Marner hadn't taken to hockey like his youngest son. He'd played mostly house league hockey until he was twelve or thirteen years old, and then switched over to competitive sailing because that was what his father was into. Paul sailed everywhere from Florida and Syracuse to California and Texas. "When you're out on ten- or sixteen-foot waves on a sixteen-foot boat and it's blowing twenty to twenty-five knots, it's very physical," said Paul. "That's why I did pretty well in races. I loved what we call heavy water and heavy wind, because I was young. The harder it blew and the bigger the waves, the more fun I had."

Paul Marner still cuts a solid physique. His wife Bonnie is more lithe. At 5-foot-9, she's the one who then-Leafs interim GM Mark Hunter joked "was a good size, so you would think [Mitch would] grow." But for years and years, Paul and Bonnie waited for Mitch to hit a growth spurt that never came. The discrepancy in size between Mitch and the other players was usually compounded by the fact that he almost always played a year up.

"When people make comments about his size, even now, I find it hilarious because he's about six feet now and about 170," said Paul Marner. "This is probably the least disadvantaged he's been his entire life to his peers. At the end of minor midget, he was 5-foot-6 and 110 pounds and when he showed up at his first OHL camp he was 5-foot-7 and 125 pounds. And everybody said, 'He'll never play.'"

Mitch Marner shoots on net while playing for the Vaughan Kings. Photo courtesy of the Marner family

The thing is, Marner always played. He always competed. His parents talk about how Mitch used to watch entire hockey games, his eyes glued to the TV, when he was ten months old. They talk about how Mitch used to not only watch games as a four-year-old, but would also point out when a player made the wrong pass. He picked up sports with ease. When he was two, he could run at full speed and kick a soccer ball with both feet.

"He picked up a lacrosse stick for the first time at five and I'm throwing him a ball and he's catching it and throwing it back to me like he'd done it before," said Paul Marner. "At the time,

Clarington was getting its first rep lacrosse team. The first year they had an A team, Mitch made the team as an under-ager and he was the only under-ager on the team."

As talented as Marner was at lacrosse, his real passion was hockey. He idolized Mats Sundin. He talked about playing in the NHL. It was all he wanted. "He'd be in the kitchen with the ministick taking shots on my mom as she was cooking," said Mitch's brother Chris. "Taking shots between her legs, acting like the oven was the goalie net." As with lacrosse, Mitch was not only good enough to play up a year, but two years. When he was six years old, he was playing against eight-year-olds. "And it was full contact back then," said Chris. "It's not like today."

Desveaux helped with that too. Since Marner was smaller than everyone else, Desveaux aimed to make him faster, quicker and more agile. "Slippery" was the word Desveaux used. "Rob helped me with that," said Marner. "He taught me skills that would help me against taller guys, and that would get me out of situations that could go wrong."

Marner learned the "spread-eagle," a skating technique where you open your legs and point one foot north and the other south, allowing you to quickly change directions to avoid an oncoming check. "When a guy is checking you, he doesn't know if you are going to go left or right," said Desveaux.

He drilled Marner on how to hold his stick in a way that gave him added balance, sort of like a walking stick. "You have to use your stick to your advantage. Most guys in the NHL don't do that. For most, it's a detriment. It causes balance problems. I watch guys with their stick and they're falling down because of it."

Marner and Desveaux did some very odd drills. For one, Desveaux would grab a gymnastics-style springboard and place it near the hash marks. Marner would skate full speed and jump off it, spinning 360 degrees in the air, and land on one foot. Desveaux would sometimes stand in the landing area, creating an obstacle for Marner to get around. Or he would pass a puck when Marner was airborne and force him to quickly grab it and get a shot on net.

"With Mitch being so light and so agile, we played to his strengths," said Desveaux. "You have to be able to get away from people. When you've got a player like him, you've got to work on things that are going to make him the best, because he's probably never going to be two hundred pounds. All that kind of nimble stuff that he could do because he was lighter and smaller, the big guys couldn't do it because it was too hard."

Desveaux also taught Marner to take a hit. Or rather, he taught him how to avoid getting hit. And he did it the hard way. By hitting him. "I'd take him into the corner and I'd hammer him and knock him on his ass," said Desveaux, laughing. "I'm 6-foot-1 and 225 pounds, so it wasn't easy for him. I used my body, but I also used checking pads, which are these soft pads that I have. And his dad would be right in the corner and I'd be laying [Mitch] out big time. He just learned to be agile. I just taught him to spin away from me and keep away from me. That's what he did. Eventually I couldn't get near him."

No one could. At least, not legally. "Twice in London he got hurt," said Paul Marner. "One guy got an eight-game suspension and one guy got a ten-game suspension. The first guy cross-checked him from behind and he hit the boards and he didn't have the puck and wasn't even expecting it. The second one was a blind-side as he rounded the net and he didn't have the puck and the guy cross-checked him in the side of the neck."

"There were a lot of teams that tried to get under his skin or try a cheap shot," said former teammate Liam Dunda. "He's a tough guy. He might not look like it, but he can stand up for himself."

THE SECOND TIME SOMEONE UNFAIRLY JUDGED MARNER because of his size was when he was seven years old. Marner had been invited to join a summer all-star team that Lindsay Hofford was putting together. But something went wrong. The coach of the team had taken one look at Marner, who was a year younger than the other kids and significantly smaller, and cut him.

Another seven-year-old was also cut. His name was McDavid. "I was like, 'Okay, I have to get involved with this,' because they were two of the best players in their generation," said Hofford.

Hofford can now laugh at the omission, which was sort of like a band manager passing on the Beatles. "You don't want your name attached to that," Hofford said of the coach, whom he refused to name in order to save him from further embarrassment. But it just goes to show you the roadblocks that even the most talented players face during their development. "It wasn't that they weren't good enough," said Hofford. "It was that usually [the all-star team] took only one underage guy and the coach had his own team so he probably wanted to take one of his own guys. It was probably easy for him to do it."

Ask what made Marner so good back then, and Hofford doesn't talk about his speed, his shot or his jaw-dropping individual skills. Rather, he mentions his smarts. Watching him on the ice was like watching Matt Damon's character in *Good Will Hunting* at the whiteboard dissecting a math equation. It was not that Marner solved every problem he faced on the ice, it was *how* he solved it.

> He was rated very low by Central Scouting. Something like third or fourth round or something crazy like that. But after he became the player he was, about one hundred people came out of the woodwork and were like, 'Oh no, I had him but I got shut down.' After the fact, everyone supposedly knew.
>
> — **LINDSAY HOFFORD, Toronto Maple Leafs amateur scout and founder of Pro Hockey Development Group**

"I'm watching a player when I'm scouting and I'm always 'Okay, here's what he should do in this situation, here's the right play,'" said Hofford. "With Mitch, even though I'd coached and done a lot of things in hockey for twenty-five years, he would make a different play than I would think he should make and it would usually be a better play than I had seen. I'm like, 'This guy is not normal.' It's not a teachable thing that he's got. And he was doing it without the physical strengths that a lot of other players have."

For a while, Marner and McDavid were at around the same level. Both played up a year and both put up gobs of points whenever they stepped on the ice. "There are a lot of similarities between the two," said Marner's agent Darren Ferris, who recruited McDavid to the Orr Hockey Group before leaving to start his own agency. "Both are great players. Different style of players, but both great players and great people. Their intelligence is off the charts."

Eventually, the gap between the two players widened. Part of it had to do with size. While McDavid hit his growth spurt and became much faster and stronger, Marner remained the same size. "Mitch was so much smaller that he had to do three strides to Connor's one at that point," said Hofford.

It wasn't just that McDavid's skate size changed. In 2012, McDavid applied for exceptional status and entered the OHL as an underage fifteen-year-old. Marner, meanwhile, was too small for that big of a jump. For the first time in his hockey career, he stayed back and played with his age group.

"We wanted him to stay up and his coach talked us into keeping him down," said Paul Marner. "In hindsight, I wish I would have had him stay up because that stigma of always being considered too small would have been erased, because you're not only playing up a year but you're also dominating a year up. That's what Connor had."

"Once you have that tag that you're small, it never goes away," said Ferris.

Marner did make some changes that year aimed at putting himself in a better light. He moved over to the GTHL and played for the Don Mills Flyers, where the competition was greater and there were far more scouts in the stands. "My feeling is he was a smaller player going into his draft year, so the family wanted to make sure he was seen for the calibre of player he was, as many parents do," said Don Mills head coach Steve Mercer.

Playing in the GTHL put more eyeballs on Marner, but it wasn't exactly a dream scenario. The Don Mills Flyers were a weak team, having rarely made the playoffs. Aside from Marner and goalie Jack LaFontaine, a third-round pick of the Carolina Hurricanes in 2016, there wasn't much else. Marner had 41 goals and 86 points in 55 games. The team's next-highest scorer, Liam Dunda, had as many points as Marner had goals.

"We really only had one and a half lines," said Dunda, a St. Louis Blues prospect. "If Mitch or I didn't score, we probably didn't have a goal that game. He had one goal where he back-checked and stripped the guy of the puck and then went up the ice and beat four guys clean and scored on his knees. We were on the bench like, 'Oh my God, I've never seen that before.' I have no idea how he did that. We would say that a lot. You can't believe your eyes."

The Flyers lost in the first round of the playoffs, but not going deep might have been the best thing for Marner. Although his season in the GTHL had ended, his playoffs were just beginning for the St. Michael's Buzzers in the Ontario Junior Hockey League. It might not have been as competitive as the OHL, but Tier 2 hockey provided Marner with experience playing against twenty-year-old men destined for the NCAA. For scouts, it was a chance to see whether Marner could handle himself against bigger and stronger players.

The Buzzers were a deep team that had played the entire season together when Marner was called up in mid-January. "I think we had thirteen scholarship kids on that team," said Buzzers head coach Rich Ricci—so Marner spent the first several games watching from the stands. He finally got in after one of the forwards suffered an injury, but at fifteen years old he was a bit player on the fourth line. It was not until the championship final against the Newmarket Hurricanes that Marner got a chance to show what he could do. The Buzzers were down 2–1 in the series when Marner picked up an assist in Game 4 and scored the game-winner in Game 5. But he saved his best performance for an all-or-nothing Game 7.

"I was excited," said Marner. "I was going to be playing a lot of minutes, but at the same time, you're nervous about being out there and making mistakes, because you don't know the team well and you don't want to screw it up. But I was a young kid. It was another game. Lucky enough, I was able to help the team."

St. Michael's College School arena, which was originally built as an outdoor arena in 1956, is located in the heart of downtown Toronto. It holds only 1,600 fans, but it can seem like there is a zero added to that number because of how close the seats are to the ice and how the domed wooden roof bounces the sound back down to the ice.

When the Buzzers returned home for Game 7, the old barn was packed for what would be the biggest game of Marner's young career. But if he was feeling pressure, he didn't let it show. A minute and nine seconds into the game, the crowd roared as Marner freed himself from a check at the side of the net and slid in a back-door pass to put St. Mike's ahead 1–0. "He was giving me looks on the bench like, you know, 'I want to get on the ice,'" said Ricci. "I said to my assistants, 'This kid's a special player.'" Ricci elevated Marner to the top line. With the Buzzers ahead 2–1 in the third period, Marner put the game out of reach by tapping in a loose puck that was lying inside the crease to make it 3–1.

"He never panicked," said Ricci. "What really stood out was our building was sold out and here comes this kid and he's making plays against twenty-year-olds in a Game 7 for the league championship. And he's being creative. He didn't change his game at all. He was creative as ever, going to the dirty areas, wanting to score goals. That game propelled him to be a first-round OHL pick, in my opinion."

Yes, but it still took some arm-twisting for it to happen. Despite what Marner had accomplished for Don Mills and St. Mike's, teams in the OHL were still unsure whether it would translate at the next level. Marner had scholarship offers from Michigan and other NCAA schools, but that was because he was still a year away from being eligible for college and would have more time to grow. As for the OHL, nobody was guaranteeing he would even be picked in the first few rounds.

"I had the guy from the Peterborough Petes call me and say 'We'd really like to draft Mitch and can we come meet with you?'" said Paul Marner. "I said, 'Where do you have him?' [He] said probably second or third round. I said, 'Don't waste your time. We're not interested. If I don't get an education package, then we're not interested.' So he came to the house and said, 'What would it take for Mitch to come to the Petes?' I said first round. They were picking fourth overall and I said that if they pick him fourth, then I have something to be interested in. He literally started giggling in front of me and said, 'You don't really believe your kid should be picked not only in the first round but a top-five pick?' I said, 'When the NHL draft rolls around in two years, I'll tell you who was right and who was wrong.'"

Peterborough ended up drafting Matthew Spencer, a 6-foot-1, 200-pound defenceman who in 2015 became a second-round pick of the Tampa Bay Lightning. Eighteen other teams also passed on Marner, mostly because he was 5-foot-7 and 130 pounds. "A lot of people thought he was trying to get to London, but at the time there weren't a lot of teams knocking on the door to take him," said Ferris. "London showed him some love and that's where he ended up." Even then, it wasn't exactly love at first sight. "There was obviously some discussion with our scouts about not taking him, because they wanted bigger guys," said Hofford, then the director of scouting for the London Knights. "There were names batted around that in hindsight would have been disastrous if we had picked them."

The Knights are one of the most storied and successful franchises in the OHL. Since Dale and Mark Hunter became co-owners in 2000, the organization has been run like an NHL team, with a pro-style arena and amenities as well as a smart and aggressive scouting staff that year after year seems to attract the brightest stars. From 2004 to 2016, the Knights finished with the most points in the OHL and won five league championships and two Memorial Cups. From Rick Nash and Corey Perry to Patrick Kane and Bo Horvat, the Knights have a reputation for turning out star NHLers. But they also have a reputation for being open-minded when it comes to looking past a player's physical shortcomings as long as his talent outweighs his actual weight.

"We tried to find these guys who were late bloomers physically, because we were always finishing near the top in London and picking later in the draft," said Hofford, who also worked as a scouting consultant with the Knights. "Size was never an issue, as long as they competed and had immense skill. Our thing was always skill." Marner, whom the Knights selected nineteenth overall, tested just how open-minded they were.

Mark Hunter, the team's co-owner and GM, wasn't the problem. He was not afraid of smaller, skilled players. But his brother Dale, who was the team's co-owner and head coach, wasn't so sure. The first time Dale Hunter went to watch Marner play,

Marner had been sick with the flu and looked every bit as small and out of his league as you would imagine the smallest player on the ice to look. With London still on the fence, Hofford asked Marner's parents if they had any game footage of Mitch that they could send to Dale. The parents smiled at each other. "How much do you need?"

"You're always worried," said Dale Hunter. "But when I saw him against twenty-year-olds who were twice his size in Junior B, I was sold. He was a special player. And that was in the playoffs too." Hunter signed off on the decision. But he also told Paul Marner not to expect his kid to play that season in London. He was still too small.

A day or two after Canada lost at the World Juniors, [Marner] flew back from Finland and had a couple of days off before he had to head back to London. He showed up at the Hill Academy just randomly. I came into the lobby, and when the kids have a break in the action from their workouts they play our version of European handball. Mitch was playing with the younger guys. And this was the day after coming back from a disappointing experience. But he just always saw the ray of sunshine in every opportunity. I think that's why he has a positive influence on others. Even in the toughest times, he's having fun.

— **PATRICK MERRILL, admissions director, Hill Academy**

ON CASUAL INSPECTION, THE game looks a lot like European handball, with a few minor changes. For one, it's played with indoor soccer nets and there's no goalie crease. You're still allowed only three steps before you have to either pass or shoot the ball, but now defenders are allowed to knock the ball out of a player's hand. But ultimately the thing that makes "Noble Ball" so unique is that hockey players play it.

"We've had a couple of people lose teeth," said Dan Noble, the athletic development coach at Toronto's Hill Academy. "We've had to dial it back a little bit."

Noble created the game when he started working at the Hill Academy in the second year of the private school's existence. At the time, there were about twenty kids enrolled at the sports academy and space was limited. He needed a game that the kids could play to break up the tedium of weight training, something that was fun but also beneficial. So he grabbed a rubber dodge ball and a couple of indoor soccer nets and created what he describes as a cross between Aussie Rules football and European handball.

"It's pretty hectic sometimes," said Marner. "But it's better than working out. When we were younger, we didn't understand the benefit it had. It was just better to play that than lift weights."

"It's become my barometer, because it demonstrates athleticism or lack thereof," said Noble. "I've always said that our top-ten Noble Ball players of all time are always the most successful athletes who have gone on to do really good things after graduating. Mitch would be top three for sure." Noble's favourite saying is "bullets over bowling balls." He wants players to be quick, agile, light on their feet, but also explosive. "Marner," said Noble, is an "F1 sports car." He's small, but he's got an engine that won't quit.

"People look at his body weight but he's probably pound for pound one of the strongest guys in the NHL," said Noble. "Yesterday, he was doing sled pushes of five hundred pounds. He's phenomenal. Strength is not an issue. If you look at his legs and watch him do a lunge or a squat, his legs are massive. Mitch is an outlier in the way his body responds to external stimulus. He picks things up very quickly and his body adapts very quickly."

A Formula One sports car was not the image that came to mind when Ryan Rupert first saw Marner take off his shirt before his first practice with the London Knights in 2013. He was more like a go-kart. "I just remember him coming into training camp and seeing how small he was. I was like, 'Who is this kid?'" said Rupert. "You could see his ribs and all his bones. I remember he and I used to go to Marble Slab together. We'd be trying to put some weight on him. He was just real, real small. But once you saw him practise and play, you knew he was going to be something special because he was so fast and so skilled."

In Marner's first season in London, the team was hosting the Memorial Cup and therefore loading up with older, more established players. On a roster that included future NHLers Max Domi, Bo Horvat, Chris Tierney and Michael McCarron, Marner wasn't promised he'd play much. But it wasn't long before he pushed his way up the depth chart, not only finishing second in rookie scoring with 59 points in 64 games, but also earning the coach's trust so much that Dale Hunter felt comfortable using him on the point on the power play.

"I always let the young guys feel their way through," said Hunter. "He just kept earning more and more ice time. He's a player. He's determined. You saw it with the Leafs as a rookie. His work ethic is outstanding, his brain is outstanding; he's just a hockey guy. He gets it. I'd ask questions to the group, like 'What happened on this play here, what was the mistake made?' And Mitch would answer right away. He's got a great hockey brain. I had to finally tell him, 'Mitch, let the other guys answer.' He's a special, special player. They don't come around much. I just loved to coach him."

Marner finished second in OHL scoring the following season—three points back from Dylan Strome—and was drafted fourth overall by the Maple Leafs, behind McDavid, Eichel and Strome. Toronto was in the early stages of a rebuild and would finish the following season with the worst overall record, so Marner was returned to London for a third season where he was told to win a Memorial Cup. "He became a leader. We saw it that year," said Dale Hunter. "Talking to the guys, he'd be 'C'mon guys, let's get it going, we're down a couple of goals.' So it really developed his leadership abilities and honed his skills."

Marner also became a winner. The Knights won 51 of 68 games in the regular season in 2015–16 and then went on a fourteen-game winning streak in the playoffs, sweeping the Kitchener Rangers, Erie Otters and Niagara IceDogs to win the OHL championship as well as the Memorial Cup. A huge part of their success was the top line of Marner, Matthew Tkachuk and Christian Dvorak, who combined scored a whopping 153 points in 22 games. "There was instant chemistry," said Tkachuk. "I think we did realize how special of an opportunity this could be and how we wanted it to work."

"He can see things out there that no one else can," said Dvorak. "I don't think we had to call much for the puck."

The following season, the player who had been underestimated for most of his life was a member of the Toronto Maple Leafs, where he exceeded everyone's expectations except his own and those of his family. "I knew what he was capable of," said Chris Marner. "I knew he would prove people wrong and always somehow be able to accomplish what he set out to do. I've been in many instances where someone has said, 'Mitch isn't going to do anything' and I've just bitten my tongue. I let people have their opinions, because at the end of the day I know what my brother is capable of."

Mark [Hunter] and I are pretty close. Will that make a difference when the draft comes around? Hey, there are no guarantees. But he knows my game, he knows what I've done and he knows what I can potentially do as I develop and get better… It's nice having someone up there who really knows you, who has taken a chance on you before and hopefully might again if the opportunity presents itself.

— **MITCH MARNER,** *Toronto Sun*, **June 2015**

MARNER WORE A BLUE TIE AND A BLUE SHIRT TO THE 2015 NHL Entry Draft in Sunrise, Florida. It was his favourite colour, he said. Plus, he wanted to match. At the time, it wasn't a foregone conclusion that the Toronto Maple Leafs were going to pick

Marner with the fourth overall pick. With McDavid, Eichel and Dylan Strome all off the board, the decision was between Marner and defenceman Noah Hanifin—an undersized winger or a safe and steady defenceman. It was not an easy choice.

The Leafs' front office was somewhat divided on who the team should choose. Some, reportedly including head coach Mike Babcock, believed that a rebuilding team was better off with a stud defenceman who could log twenty-plus minutes a night. Others apparently agreed. NHL Central Scouting had Hanifin ranked third among North American skaters, with Marner ranked sixth, right behind 6-foot-4, 212-pound winger Lawson Crouse.

But something had occurred three weeks before the draft that tipped the scales in Marner's favour. A day after finishing the season with the fourth-worst record in the NHL, the Leafs purged most of their front office staff, firing general manager Dave Nonis, interim head coach Peter Horachek and his entire coaching staff, as well as sixteen members of the scouting department. Even the team's video co-ordinator was let go.

The biggest change? Mark Hunter, who less than a year earlier had been hired as the Leafs' director of player personnel, was named interim general manager, giving him control of the draft. Others around the league might have been gun-shy about taking a 5-foot-10 winger who tipped the scales at 160 pounds, but Hunter—and Lindsay Hofford, who had been hired on as a new scout—weren't fooled so easily. After all, when they had first drafted Marner, he was only 5-foot-7 and 125 pounds. "You've seen this young man at fifteen and now he's grown into a man," said Hunter.

"He had no doubt in me then and it looks like he has no doubt in me now," Marner said at the time. "If you would have told me that he would have drafted me in the NHL and the OHL at the same time, I wouldn't have believed you. But weird things happen like this and it's a special thing to happen." You could say the same thing about Marner's development.

Auston MATTHEWS

TORONTO MAPLE LEAFS
» № 34 «

POSITION	CENTRE
SHOOTS	LEFT
HEIGHT	6'3"
WEIGHT	216 LB
BORN	SEPTEMBER 17, 1997
BIRTHPLACE	SAN RAMON, CA, USA
DRAFT	2016 TOR, 1ST RD, 1ST PK (1ST OVERALL)

Auston Matthews (left) and William Nylander celebrate a goal.

The Canadian Press/Frank Gunn

O NE NIGHT IN OCTOBER, AUSTON MATTHEWS EMBAR-
rassed a two-time Norris Trophy winner and scored four
goals. It was his first NHL game. And it was equal parts
magic and in Matthews's words, "surreal," the kind of thing you
expect to see in a feel-good sports movie, right down to the shots
of Matthews's mom Ema in the stands, her face a mixture of joy,
pride and surprise. The only thing missing was the win, although
the fact that a nineteen-year-old rookie scored all four goals in a
5–4 loss was a sure-fire sign that the Toronto Maple Leafs' for-
tunes were about to change.

The rebuild was over. The pain had been lifted. The saviour
had finally arrived.

As Leafs head coach Mike Babcock told reporters, "We were
all a part of history. I've never seen anything like that." Indeed,
most players' "Welcome to the NHL" moment involves getting
caught with their heads down and receiving a big hit or cough-
ing up the puck and getting burned for a goal against. But in his
much-anticipated debut, the first overall draft pick flipped the
script. Matthews welcomed everyone to his world and in the process taught the league a few lessons.

Lesson No. 1: Matthews is fast. On his first-ever goal, the
Leafs centre beat a couple of slow-footed Ottawa Senators forwards to the front of the net and one-timed a pass that sailed over
outstretched goaltender Craig Anderson.

Auston MATTHEWS

Lesson No. 2: Matthews is a thief. After deking past a couple of defenders, Matthews briefly lost the puck to all-star defenceman Erik Karlsson, whom Matthews then hunted down and promptly took the puck back from, before beating Anderson with a shot through his legs for his second goal.

Lesson No. 3: Matthews can shoot. Parked just below the hash marks in the soft spot of Ottawa's defence, Matthews took a pass from Morgan Rielly and in one quick motion fired it into the back of the net to complete his hat trick.

Lesson No. 4: Matthews can do it all. On a play that showcased everything in his tool box, Matthews broke up a shot on the backcheck, used his speed to race up the ice and then played give-and-go with Nylander before scoring his fourth goal with three seconds remaining in the second period.

"He got four scoring chances and he scored four goals," Karlsson told reporters in Ottawa afterward. "Two of them, most people probably can't do. Good for him and good for Toronto for having a player like that." Even Senators goalie Craig Anderson was impressed. After the game, he asked for one of Matthews's game-used sticks, which the Leafs rookie cheekily signed, *Thanks 'FOUR' making the first game memorable.* "It's probably going to be a National Hockey League record for as long as I'm alive," Anderson told reporters.

If Matthews's NHL debut was memorable, his journey to the NHL was nothing short of improbable. Most hockey players are born in cold climates, spend their winters skating on frozen ponds or backyard rinks, and are fed through the traditional development stream of playing major junior hockey in Canada or the NCAA in the United States. But then along comes Matthews. He was born in California and raised in Arizona. He learned how to play hockey in the desert, on a tiny three-on-three rink no bigger than a football field's end zone. He didn't go to college. He didn't play major junior.

Instead, after shattering Patrick Kane's single-season scoring record in the US National Development Team Program, Matthews did what no one had done before him and jetted off to Switzerland to play professionally during his NHL draft year. Ultimately, he ended up in Toronto, the so-called centre of the hockey universe, as the first overall pick of an Original Six franchise. "It's a crazy story," said Matthews. "I didn't do it to be a trailblazer or a trend-setter. I just did it because I thought it was the best path for me."

THE EXTRAORDINARY STORY of how Matthews became the first overall pick in the NHL began with an uncle who happened to buy a pair of season tickets to the city's newest professional sports team. The Winnipeg Jets had relocated to

> It speaks volumes of all the people who have put so much work in to developing hockey in Arizona. To have a talent like that come out of here is a credit to them.
> — **DAVID TIPPETT, former head coach of the Arizona Coyotes, 2016**

Arizona a year before Matthews was born. The first time he went to a game, he sat on his father's lap for free, paying more attention to the Zamboni, which he called *el trucké*, and to the remote-controlled balloons that dropped parachuted T-shirts from the rafters, than to the actual players.

Matthews's mom Ema grew up in a family of nine children on a ranch in Hermosillo, Mexico. When she met Brian Matthews while working as a flight attendant, she didn't even know how to speak English, much less know anything about hockey. Matthews's father Brian was only slightly more interested in the game. He was born in California and had pitched in college before his arm blew out as a junior. He didn't learn to skate until he was in his thirties. "I got to where I can skate forward and backward, turn, do all that stuff," he said. "I just fell in love with the game as [Auston] fell in love with it."

175

Matthews was a Coyotes fan at a perfect time, when the buzz around the brand-new franchise was strong and the team was actually winning more games than they were losing. The Coyotes made the playoffs in five of their first six seasons and had star players like Jeremy Roenick and Keith Tkachuk on the roster. Matthews, who received a Daniel Briere jersey as a Christmas present when he was six years old, was hooked. "It was pretty much the hottest thing," Matthews said of the Coyotes. "I don't think we had the NFL and the basketball team was not doing well. To have a new team come in was a pretty hot topic, especially with the players like Roenick and Tkachuk."

Auston Matthews and his family attend a Phoenix Coyotes game. At Auston's first game, he was more interested in the Zamboni and the remote-controlled balloons that dropped parachuted T-shirts from the rafters than the game, but by the time he was six, he was a huge Coyotes fan. Photo courtesy of the Matthews family

Turning a hockey fan into a hockey player, however, was almost as difficult as growing grass in the desert. Hockey wasn't baseball, which Brian Matthews understood. And it wasn't golf, which was literally in their backyard. There was no template, no previous examples of what worked and what didn't. In some ways, that worked to the Matthews's advantage. Brian Matthews didn't feel the same pressure that Canadians feel when enrolling their kids in hockey. He didn't follow any guidelines, because there weren't any. Instead, he started writing his own learner's manual, implementing ideas from other sports and questioning every rule that the hockey traditionalists threw his way.

"Brian is a smart man and is willing to think outside the box and understand the upside and the opportunities his son is going through and what Auston can bring to the game as well," said Pat Brisson, Matthews's agent. "Auston's fortunate to have such great parents."

The first obstacle: cost. Ice was hard to come by in Arizona, so because of that it was really expensive. When Matthews was three years old, his mom pushed back the C-section birth of his sister by an hour so he wouldn't miss his first hockey practice and essentially toss money down the drain. As Matthews got older and played at higher levels, the costs multiplied. "It's not like you're living in Detroit and you're driving a couple of hours to play somewhere else in Michigan. Or if you're in Boston or New York or something," said Brian. "Everything was like an adventure. As you look for better and better competition, you have to head out east. There's a cost element, there's a time element."

Auston Matthews attends a hockey clinic in Arizona. He had many coaches over the years, including Boris Dorozhenko. Photo courtesy of the Matthews family

The Matthews family sacrificed. Ema worked two jobs—at Starbucks and as a waitress—to help pay for their son's passion. But they also found out a way to feed their son's insatiable appetite for more and more hockey, while at the same time allowing Matthews to practically skate for free. Matthews lived about a ten-minute drive from Ozzie Ice, a dual-rink facility that had one ice pad and one synthetic pad that were about one-third the size of a regulation rink. Aside from games of pickup hockey, Ozzie Ice was mostly used as a training rink. That is, until Brian, who volunteered at the rink, suggested creating a three-on-three league.

"It exploded," he said. "I mean, who doesn't want to play in a league where the score is 48–45?" Since Brian was helping out with the league—running the score clock, and making sure the officials showed up and the teams had a goalie and enough players—his son also hung around and helped out. Inevitably, a team would be short a player and Auston would ask if he could fill in. "Sure," said his father. "Just grab a jersey and go."

"We'd skate all day," recalled Brian. "It was ideal for me and ideal for Auston. He'd be smoked by the time he got home, but with a big grin on his face because he got to skate all day and score a lot of goals." The beauty of playing three-on-three meant there were more opportunities to touch the puck and more opportunities to score goals than in traditional games. It was also non-contact, so Matthews could play with bigger and older kids. Some laughed at the type of hockey that was being played, with scores resembling a football game, but for a young player still developing his stickhandling and skating skills, it had obvious advantages over skating up and down a full rink, sometimes going an entire game without actually touching the puck.

"A lot of the skills I've developed today are from that," Matthews said of Ozzie Ice. "It was my own little backyard rink. I was there constantly. I had every team's jersey so I could fill in and play for them and have fun. I'd be there all the time." Two things came out of those on-ice sessions: Matthews developed a knack for scoring goals, and because the ice surface was about one-third the size of a regulation rink, he learned how to stickhandle in an area the size of a phone booth.

"You watch him in the pre-game skate and he takes the puck and stickhandles just on the faceoff dot," said Mark Ciaccio, a former skills coach with the Arizona Coyotes. "That's all he's doing. He's doing all these different stickhandling moves on the dot and it's such a small area. That comes from playing in three-on-three. He was always good at working in tight areas. His stickhandling skills are unbelievable." When Matthews showed up at tournaments as a fill-in player on the bigger ice surface, the extra space and extra time made him twice as dangerous. It was like taking batting practice against a pitcher who is standing half the distance from home plate and then suddenly having an extra thirty feet to see the ball coming in during actual games. It was too easy.

"It's no different than what the Brazilians do," said Brian Matthews. "They have a small soccer game that they play in Brazil—it's huge. It forces skill development and it forces [them] to learn how to dribble the ball and all those things. It's no different than three-on-three. [Auston] had to learn very quickly where to go. It's not just the skills with the puck, but without the puck, knowing where to put yourself so you can get the puck and where you can put yourself in a position to score. That sort of thing helps. And then when you go to the big ice, you're like, 'Oh my gosh, look at all this space I have now.' And it just opens up a whole other world for you. I think maybe it helped slow the game down even more for him."

Most other hockey parents didn't think this way, because this wasn't the way they had learned how to play hockey. But Brian Matthews wasn't like other hockey parents. There was no blueprint. Instead, he was self-proclaimed "the crazy Arizonian who looked at things differently than everyone else." That line of thinking is how Auston Matthews ended up with Boris Dorozhenko as a power skating coach.

Dorozhenko was born in Ukraine and had been coaching the Mexican national team, which is something you don't see on most skating coaches' resumés. By his own admission, he is "a crazy guy" who teaches an even crazier technique that emphasizes balance and control but in ways that few can imagine. There were no pucks at a typical Dorozhenko practice. There was no time spent on systems training or scrimmaging. It was just hours and hours of skating. "I always say as far as the edges go, Boris is pretty hard to beat," said Ron Filion, one of Matthews's first coaches. "But the method is very out there and it's not for everyone."

For five to six hours a week, Matthews performed huge leaps and pirouettes, ran in circles, stomped his feet and tried not to fall down while balancing on his heels for minutes at a time. It looked ridiculous, and some parents told Brian Matthews that he was wasting his money and his son's time. But those were typical hockey parents. The Matthews family was not trying to be typical. "Everything is very unique," Auston said of Dorozhenko's methods. "It's all edgework and you do jumps and 360s in the air. You're wondering 'What the heck is this?' But then you go into a corner and you're spinning off guys so easily and you start to realize that's kind of how it all works together and translates to the game. Looking at it from the outside, I know people were wondering what we were doing. But if you go into it with an open mind and work hard at it, I think it's a really good option."

In Dorozhenko, who was invited to live at the Matthews's home for two years and essentially became part of the family, Brian Matthews found someone with a similar outlook. He wasn't afraid to try new things, to admit that the old way wasn't always the right way. In Auston Matthews, Dorozhenko found a student with natural skill but also with a sense of adventure. One year, Dorozhenko convinced Brian Matthews to put Auston on the worst team in the state, because he would get more ice time and learn leadership qualities. Another year, Dorozhenko took Auston to a tournament in Quebec City—as part of an all-Ukrainian team.

"He was always my showman, because my style is very different," said Dorozhenko. "Every day we were changing drills—some didn't work, some were a waste of time—but Auston was trying them all. He didn't complain. We would skate three hours on the ice and afterward he'd be shooting pucks on net. He had such energy, such passion. He's a gamer.

"I started working with him when he was eight years old and he was really just making his first step on the ice. Auston was very competitive right from the beginning. He hated to be second. He had to be first. It helped him a lot. Some of the drills I do are very hard for beginners. I remember one particular drill, he was almost crying because he couldn't do it. I asked him to quit or to have a break for fifteen minutes. But he said no and kept trying and trying until he got it. When he felt not satisfied with a drill, he would keep doing it again and again."

The results were so good that Brian Matthews eventually pulled his son out of Triple-A and put him in a lower level, where there were fewer games, just so he could spend more time working with Dorozhenko. A year later, Brian signed his son up for Triple-A, but only as a practice player so he could learn proper positioning. Again, it was something no one else was doing. "I don't know many kids that could take a year off," said Filion. "But at the end of the day, not everyone is Auston Matthews."

"It wasn't because he couldn't play Triple-A hockey," said Brian. "He was playing up an age level. But I wanted the training; I wanted the development. It was at that nine-, ten-, eleven-, twelve-, thirteen-year-old range where I needed development; I needed skill development. To Auston's credit, he hated it, but he bought into it. Believe me, he was bitching. There was so much skating, so much edge work, so much stickhandling. But he saw the results, because when he would go to Triple-A tournaments, he was like, 'Wow, it's easy to go around this guy or do this move.' So there was, for lack of a better word, affirmation for what he was going through."

WALK THROUGH THE FRONT DOOR OF THE HOME WHERE Matthews grew up and you'll notice a sign hanging on the wall: *Peace is not about Silence. It's not a place where there is no trouble or fear. Peace is standing in the middle of that chaos and finding a calmness in your heart.*

Brian Matthews put the sign up when the kids were young. It's a constant reminder that you cannot always control the outside noise and distractions in life, but what you can control is how you handle them. Stay calm, stay focused and make things happen. "That's what the great ones do," said Brian. "The easy times are easy. When you're scoring a hat trick and the puck just seems to be going in no matter what you do, life's grand. But when the tough stuff happens, that's when you can see who you are. That's why some players are labelled great."

THE US NATIONAL TEAM DEVELOPMENT PROGRAM (NTDP), located in Plymouth, Michigan, has graduated many talented players to the NHL over the years, including first-overall picks Patrick Kane and Erik Johnson, as well as Phil Kessel, James van Riemsdyk and Eichel. It's a sort of Hogwarts for the country's top hockey players. Admission is severely limited. There is an under-17 team and an under-18 team. And that's it.

Although everyone in Arizona's tiny hockey community knew Matthews had talent, to the rest of the hockey world he was still a bit of an unknown. "He was a natural athlete who was very good in Arizona," said Brisson. "Had he grown up in Toronto and been dominant early, there wouldn't have been a question."

When Matthews was really young, he once travelled to Toronto to play in a hockey tournament, where his team faced off against Connor McDavid's team in the final. "I'll never forget, Connor came down and in typical Connor fashion he blew by everyone on the ice and scored a highlight reel goal," said Brian Matthews. "And the parents were like, 'That's our kid.'" But the one-man show quickly turned into a duel. "Auston came down and while he didn't have the same speed, he deked around every one of their guys and scored a highlight reel goal. Our team's parents turned around and said, 'Well, that's our kid.' And the other parents were kind of like shaking their heads like, 'Well, okay.'"

It was like that for most of his career. Some might have heard that there was a player from the desert who was really good at hockey. But no one really believed he was the best. After all, how good do you have to be to play hockey in Arizona?

Auston Matthews goes for the puck while playing for the Junior Coyotes. Photo courtesy of the Matthews family

It was only after Matthews scored 55 goals and 100 points in 48 games with the Triple-A Arizona Bobcats—he picked up his one hundredth point on the final shift of his last game—that he was invited to the NTDP tryouts.

"He flew in to see the program and we had him on the ice with the 1995s," said Don Granato, who was then the head coach of the NTDP. "On that same team I had [fifth overall pick in 2015] Noah Hanifin and [eighth overall pick in 2015] Zach Werenski and ten first-round picks. But Auston walked in and he was totally different."

If Matthews looked out of place, it wasn't because he couldn't keep up to the rest of the players. Rather, no one could keep up with him.

"He'd never had exposure to high-end talent, but his skill level was unreal," said Granato. "I remember walking up to our scouting co-ordinator after and saying, 'You do have him signed, don't you? He doesn't need a tryout.'"

Granato may have been impressed, but the players on the ice were in shock. Most of them knew each other, had played against one another in tournaments, and here was this unknown kid from Arizona who schooled them all. "He was a kid that wasn't a name yet," said Matthew Tkachuk, now a forward with the Calgary Flames. "He was in Arizona and not many people knew about him. I remember we got to playing and—I might be over-exaggerating but if I am it's not by much—he had like fifteen goals in the tryout. He really opened the eyes of everybody. He basically showed all the coaches there and all the players that he was the best player and it wasn't close. It was really cool to see a guy that no one really knew about just come out of nowhere and take over."

Soon after Auston's tryout, Granato picked up the phone and called Brian Matthews. He wanted to report on how Auston had performed, but more importantly he wanted to warn him: "Get ready for your life to be crazy." In other words, the kid was exceptional. Matthews didn't just fit in. He blew away the competition. He was the best skater, was the best stickhandler, had the best shot and, according to Granato, had a "purity" about him that seemed destined for stardom. "This is the only conversation I've had with a parent like that," said Granato. "I felt it was necessary to bring to Brian's attention right away that his life's going to get pretty crazy. I remember asking, 'Brian, do you have any idea how good Auston is?' And he kind of chuckled and said, 'No, I have no idea. That's why he's with you. We don't know these things.'"

Matthews began the year on the U-17 team, but he missed three months of the season because of a broken left femur. At that age, the injury should have hurt his development. Instead, he somehow came back even stronger than before and was asked to play up a year, winning his first of two gold medals at the U-18 world championship with a five-goal performance that tied for the most goals on the team. "He was supposed to be out for most of the year and he came back before Christmas," said Tkachuk, "and he started to score all these goals and quickly became our best player. Just when you think you know a player, he gets that much better."

The following season, 2014–15, was even more unreal. Matthews scored 55 goals and 117 points in 60 games. He also won a second gold with the American team at the 2015 U-18 World Championship and captured bronze at the 2016 World Junior Championship while tying for the tournament lead with seven goals. "He has such an enormous appetite for more and more," said Granato. "The fun thing for me was challenging him. There were times in a game where I'd go down the bench and say to him, 'Hey, you've got to have a better shift.' Even if he had a great shift he would give you a snarl, like, 'That wasn't good enough? Okay, I'll give you something.' And he was phenomenal at that. I'd go walk the other way on the bench and say to my assistant, 'Watch, Auston's going to score now.' I probably did that ten times during our U-18 year and within two or three shifts he scored or set up Matthew Tkachuk or Jack Roslovic for a goal."

If his in-game performance was something to behold, his practice habits were legendary. First on and last off, but it was more than hard work and maximum effort. Granato often tells stories about how even during scrimmages the rest of the team would stop and watch, simply because you never knew what amazing thing he would do next. "Again, we had Hanifin and Werenski out there and plenty of talent," said Granato. "But when Auston picked the puck up, kids didn't know it but they all got up off the bench and leaned forward to see what he would do."

If Auston Matthews wants to play on the moon or in Uzbekistan it doesn't matter. He's a stud player. [Playing in Europe is] not going to change his draft place.

— **CRAIG BUTTON, TSN's director of scouting**

COMING OUT OF THE NTDP, Matthews had a lot of options. He could play in the Western Hockey League (the Everett Silvertips had his rights) or the NCAA (as many as five different schools had recruited him). But none of these options were what he really wanted to do, which was to play in the NHL. The problem was he was born two days after the cut-off date for the NHL Entry Draft, which meant unlike McDavid and Eichel, who were born in the same year as Matthews, he had to wait another twelve months to join the league.

That's how playing in Switzerland came up. He didn't necessarily want to be different. But he wanted a challenge.

"I just saw it as a pretty good opportunity for myself to play against men in a pro league," said Matthews. "Like I said, it's a skilled league and it's fast and I really wanted to challenge myself." Matthews's father had actually looked into Europe a couple of years earlier when debating whether the NTDP was right for Auston—again, those crazy Arizonians and their crazy ideas—but was talked out of it.

There were obvious concerns. The Swiss game was unlike the NHL game. The ice was bigger and the league was less physical. Even top Swiss players, like 2017 first overall pick Nico Hischier, come to North America and play in the CHL before their draft year.

"People were telling us what are you doing, you're sending him to the bigger ice surface in Europe, it's not going to be good for his development," said Brisson. "But there are a lot of Europeans who grew up playing on the large surfaces who come here and they don't do too badly. This kid grew up in North America. One year's not going to kill him. Besides, the Swiss league is better."

It was when Matthews went to the U-18 championship in Lucerne that the idea of playing professionally in Switzerland took shape. After the tournament, in which the US beat Finland for gold and Matthews was named tournament MVP, the Matthews family flew to Zurich where they met with Zurich Lions head coach Marc Crawford. "He wanted Auston—he wanted to develop him. He had seen him play and had a firm understanding of what Auston could do and what he would focus on and how it would go," said Brian. "[Crawford] wasn't going to baby him, but push him to be the best player he could be against men in an NHL-type setting. It kind of all fit."

Deciding on Switzerland was the easy part. Getting Matthews into a game proved to be the biggest challenge. He was repeatedly denied a work visa. His agents tried everything and explored every avenue. At one point, the team and Brisson looked into whether Matthews would have a better chance at being accepted if he were an employee at Coca-Cola in Switzerland. Nothing worked, until someone with the US Embassy suggested Matthews get his high school diploma, which meant taking a high school equivalency test. "It was not an easy process. There were so many layers," said Brian. "That was probably the roughest two to three months as a family, because we knew it was the right thing for him, but it was out of our control. As soon as we thought we had it, here would come another hurdle and another hurdle. And it taxed everybody. There were times where all of us were thinking, what's next? Maybe this is not to be. But we just kept pushing forward."

It was worth it. Some might have wondered whether Switzerland was the right place to develop a player who was headed to the NHL, but it provided Matthews with a different experience. "I remember talking to John Tavares and Patrick Kane, who both played there during the lockout, and they said, 'This is a great league,'" said Brisson. "It's great for your skills. It's not easy. You've got to skate; you've got to have hands or you're going to be exposed. Don't take it for granted. You're playing against pros."

Matthews missed the first four games of the season—he was not allowed to play in the league before his eighteenth birthday on September 17—but he made up for lost time. He scored in his first game, with eventual totals of 24 goals and 46 points in 36 games. Despite missing fourteen games due to injury, he finished tenth in scoring. He won the Swiss league's Rising Star of the Year Award and finished second in MVP voting behind a thirty-one-year-old, Pierre-Marc Bouchard, who had played eleven years and scored 356 points in the NHL. "Most of the other number-one centres can't match Auston's size and don't carry their speed like he does," said Crawford. "You would be hard-pressed to come to our games and not notice him."

The Swiss league, which is played on an Olympic-sized ice surface and features a wide-open, pass-first game more reminiscent of soccer, might not have prepared Matthews for the physicality of the NHL. But playing against established pros who were older and stronger was more of a challenge than playing against his peers in college or major junior. It was the challenge Matthews had been seeking. And it came with the pressures of being a pro—where jobs rather than scholarships are on the line. "It's a better league than the AHL," said Crawford, who returned to the NHL as an assistant coach with the Ottawa Senators the year after Auston left. "The Rochester Americans were in the Spengler Cup last year and they just couldn't compete against the Swiss teams. They didn't have enough skill."

As for Matthews's draft ranking, playing in Switzerland didn't hurt him one bit. In fact, playing against men was part of the reason why Matthews was able to seamlessly join Team North America at the World Cup of Hockey before he had even made his NHL debut. "Auston was ready. He was ready for the NHL. Of course he was," said Brisson. "He would have been in the NHL had he been born two days earlier. That's why when people ask me if [playing in Europe] is going to be a trend—of course it's not. You'd have to be a late birthday, and a bigger kid physically, and so talented, or else forget about it. There's only a handful of players that could ever do this. A McDavid or an Eichel. You have to be special. It's not for everyone."

PAIN WAS COMING. THAT WAS THE WARNING BABCOCK HAD issued to fans upon his hire on May 20, 2015. As some had joked at the time, you mean it's going to get even worse? The Leafs had already been suffering more than any franchise in the NHL before the arrivals of team president Brendan Shanahan, GM Lou Lamoriello and Babcock, having not won a Stanley Cup or even reached the finals since 1967. In a ten-year span from 2005 until 2016, the team had qualified for the playoffs just once. It was not unusual for fans to show up to games with paper bags over their heads or to toss jerseys—or even food—onto the ice.

And now, in order to get better, the team was going to have to find a new rock bottom.

In other words, it was time to tank. The Leafs knew that the best way to rebuild a team was with young, talented players. That meant getting a top draft pick. And ultimately, it meant finishing with the worst record.

Upon Babcock's arrival, the team traded top scorer Phil Kessel for a package of picks and prospects. As the 2015–16 season wore on, more bodies were pushed to the side as the Leafs parted ways with captain Dion Phaneuf, Shawn Matthias, Daniel Winnik, Roman Polak, Nick Spaling and goalie James Reimer.

It worked. Toronto won just 29 games—two less than the next-worst teams—and entered the 2016 NHL Draft Lottery with a 20 per cent chance of winning the No. 1 overall pick.

"It's just good fortune," Shanahan told reporters after winning the lottery. "I think it gives our fans hope," Babcock told the *Toronto Sun.*

At that point, no one within the organization had indicated that they were picking Matthews over Finland's Patrik Laine, a talented winger who was considered the second-best prospect. At the same time, for a franchise that had been searching for a No. 1 centre ever since Mats Sundin's departure in 2008, Matthews seemed like the obvious choice.

In the months leading up to the draft, Matthews reaffirmed the scouting reports with his play at the Ice Hockey World Championship in Russia. In a tournament that is mostly made up of NHLers who are out of the playoffs, Matthews and Laine were named to their respective teams as exceptions. And both played exceptionally well.

Laine won tournament MVP after leading Finland to the championship final. Matthews, meanwhile, had an equally impressive tournament by scoring 6 goals and 9 points in 10 games for an inferior US team that had less at its disposal.

Veteran forward Nick Foligno compared Matthews to Chicago Blackhawks captain Jonathan Toews. Another called him "The Man," which was sort of ironic considering he was still a teenager and the youngest player on the team. Of course, he didn't look it.

"I don't think you can question anything about Auston Matthews," said Foligno.

PETER CHIARELLI, TEAM NORTH AMERICA'S GM, WAS SKEP-
tical. Actually, doubtful might be a better word. When asked what
type of impact he expected Matthews to make at the World Cup of
Hockey, where the nineteen-year-old was the second-youngest
player in the tournament, he was not optimistic. A year earlier,
McDavid had needed the first month of the season to figure out
the NHL and feel comfortable as the No. 1 overall pick. So it made
sense at the time that Matthews, who had not yet played a game
in the NHL, would experience a similar learning curve. "That's the
instinct in my gut," said Chiarelli. Then again, Chiarelli has
learned not to always trust his gut. It's been wrong before.

When Chiarelli and the
rest of Team North America's
management team started
writing down potential players for the World Cup roster,
Matthews's name was at or near
the bottom of the list. After all,
the league was full of star players aged twenty-three or younger.
Players who, like Canadian-born
McDavid and Ekblad or Eichel and Gaudreau of the US, would
have been good enough to represent their country had they been
given the chance. Matthews wasn't even playing in the NHL.
According Chiarelli, it would be "an uphill battle" for Matthews
to make the team.

> He got better every game. We've talked about his maturity level, his skill set, the way he plays the game. He's physical. In baseball, they call it a five-tool player. That's Auston.
>
> — **TODD MCLELLAN, Team North America head coach**

And then Matthews went to the world championship, where
as the youngest and only undrafted player on the team he scored
6 goals and 9 points in 10 games. "It was just too hard to ignore,"
said Chiarelli. "He played too well. He had a hell of a tournament
against world-class players."

Still, when the Team North America announced its final
roster, Matthews was listed as the thirteenth forward. No one

expected him to play, much less land a spot on the top line with McDavid and Scheifele. But just as with the NTDP and in Switzerland, Matthews's skill changed minds in a hurry. "Auston is a very gifted player," said head coach Todd McLellan. "He gets better every day. As we built the team, we didn't know whether he was going to be a part of it. After he made the team, he came in and we weren't sure where we were going to play him, likely as the thirteenth forward. He worked his way up, and he just keeps getting better and better."

When Matthews made his Air Canada Centre debut at the World Cup of Hockey in Toronto, most would have been impressed if he had just got into a game for Team North America. After all, this was a team that had some of the best young players in the NHL—players who had not only been top picks but had followed that up with Calder Memorial Trophy rookie seasons and were already impact players in the NHL. Instead, Matthews gave a glimpse of things to come.

On his first shift of the World Cup of Hockey, Matthews stripped Finland's Laine of the puck and then fed McDavid down the ice for an odd-man rush. On his third shift, the 6-foot-3 forward avoided a check, drove to the net and fired off a shot, with Eichel potting in the ensuing rebound to give North America a 1–0 lead.

"There was no fear in him," said McLellan. "He hasn't played his first NHL game, but he's an NHL player. He belongs. There's no, 'Let's babysit him.' Let him play. He's got all the skills and he's playing the right way. He fits."

Two games later, Matthews added another clip to his highlight reel when he deked past Sweden's Victor Hedman while on his knees before sliding a pass to Scheifele and then potting in the rebound for another goal. "He's doing stuff that elite guys are doing and he's doing it every game," Chiarelli said of Matthews. "If there's a wild card in this tournament, it's him."

If there had been trepidation in having Matthews on the team, it was immediately erased. It didn't matter that he hadn't yet played in the NHL. He more than belonged among the best.

Nor was it surprising that Matthews finished the World Cup tournament with 2 goals and 3 points in 3 games.

SHANAHAN WAS CAREFUL NOT to call Matthews a saviour when the Leafs drafted him. But it was difficult not to think of him that way on the night of his four-goal debut, especially if you were playing hockey in Arizona.

Filion, who was born in Quebec and moved to Arizona in the early 1990s, had been running hockey practice at AZ Ice Arcadia in the Desert Palms Power Center in Phoenix, Arizona just as Matthews was enjoying his historic night. The rink is the same one that Matthews skated on as a kid. And though Matthews was now playing hockey on the other side of the continent, he might as well have been playing in his hometown.

"Coach Ron! Coach Ron!" the kids shouted when they skated onto the ice on that Wednesday night in October. "Papi just scored a goal!"

Papi is Matthews's childhood nickname. And much to Filion's pleasure and annoyance, he couldn't get through a drill without hearing Papi's name. Parents, who were watching the Leafs game on a TV in the arena restaurant, banged on the glass and held up two fingers to signal to Filion that Matthews had scored a second goal. When he completed the hat trick in the second period, the entire rink erupted in cheers.

> He has done more in one night for hockey in Arizona than the Coyotes ever did. This is our kid. He's from our state. Everybody is jumping on the Auston Matthews bandwagon.
>
> **— RON FILION, Arizona Bobcats head coach**

So by the time Matthews broke the record for goals in an NHL debut and scored his fourth of the game, Filion had already given up on the practice and was standing in front of a TV with everyone else.

"At some point, it was hard for me to concentrate on the ice. I was just waiting for the next update," Filion, who had coached Matthews from when he was ten years old until he was fourteen, told the *Toronto Sun*. "The whole rink was buzzing. A lot of people, instead of watching their own kids, went to the bar, which is attached to the rink, and were watching him."

"When I was [those kids'] age, there were guys from Arizona that I was looking up to as well," said Matthews. "It's pretty special."

Well, not exactly. No one from Arizona has done what Matthews has already done. With the exception of Dave Spina, who grew up in Mesa, Arizona, and went on to play in the minors and professionally in Europe, no one even came close. It's why what Matthews has done is so special.

"I would definitely say the rise in hockey interest in Arizona recently is because of him," said Christian Cakebread, who played on the same Bobcats team as Matthews and is now at Niagara University. "There really wasn't much of a hockey scene before him. The rink that I'd go to would have like one summer camp and the ice would be open for hours on end. Now, it's exploded. Especially with the younger kids; when Auston came back the year before he was drafted it was just ridiculous the amount of people that came out there to watch him skate."

That bandwagon is bound to get more crowded. Whereas the Coyotes inspired Matthews to play hockey, having a homegrown star is bound to inspire many more to pick up the sport. According to the *Arizona Republic*, hockey registration in the state has already jumped from 2,349 during the 1996–97 season to 7,329 for the 2014–15 campaign—an increase of 312 per cent. In 2015, Filion led players born in 2002 to the peewee championship in Quebec, where the Arizona Bobcats topped thirty-one other teams to win the end-of-year tournament. This is no longer a non-traditional hockey market. If the Coyotes helped introduce the sport, then Matthews is the one who put it on the map. For kids growing up, he is the inspiration.

"We couldn't even have two Triple-A teams when Auston was playing here. And now, we were doing tryouts this weekend and we had eighty to ninety kids trying out," said Filion. "That would have been impossible even when Auston was here. We'd be lucky to get thirty kids trying out. Now, it's loaded."

Indeed, Matthews might not have followed the traditional path in order to get to the NHL, but from developing on three-on-three rinks and playing his draft year in Switzerland, he certainly blazed a trail for the next kid coming from Arizona or a place where hockey is not a dominant sport. As Matthews has said, "It's a crazy story." And it's just getting started. "I guess there's a lot of paths to the NHL," said Matthews. "Everybody's different. Obviously my path has been a little bit unique, but everybody's in the NHL for the same reason. I wanted to get to the NHL and I was going to do everything to get there, regardless of where I was from."

Patrik LAINE

WINNIPEG JETS
» № 29 «

POSITION	RIGHT WING
SHOOTS	RIGHT
HEIGHT	6'5"
WEIGHT	206 LB
BORN	APRIL 19, 1998
BIRTHPLACE	TAMPERE, FIN
DRAFT	2016 WPG, 1ST RD, 2ND PK (2ND OVERALL)

Winnipeg Jets' Patrik Laine shoots on the Edmonton Oilers during the pre-season in 2016. Notice the elasticity of his stick. The Canadian Press/ Trevor Hagan

O N THE NIGHT OF THE 2016 NHL DRAFT LOTTERY IN April, Sportsnet arranged satellite interviews with Matthews and Patrik Laine—the projected first and second overall picks in the upcoming draft—who were both in Finland preparing for the Ice Hockey World Championship held the following month in Russia. Matthews went first. Speaking from a hotel ballroom in Helsinki, Matthews sat with perfect posture and answered each question as seriously and politically correctly as possible. There were few *ums*, few *ahs*, and not much in terms of sound bites.

And then it was Laine's turn. He too was at a hotel in Helsinki, but that was where the similarities between Matthews and him ended. When Laine's picture popped up on the screen, he was lying on his back in bed, wearing a plain white T shirt with Apple car buds dangling down his chest, his eyes drifting to the ceiling. With his long blond hair and carefree smile, he gave off the impression of a laid-back California surfer dude who had just woken from a nap—something that he reinforced once he began to speak.

When asked for the secret behind his blistering slapshot, Laine said his father had hung Coke bottles in the backyard for him to break. When asked about the comparisons to Matthews, Laine matter-of-factly said, "I know that the gap is smaller." And when asked if he thought it was possible he could leapfrog Matthews and go first in the draft, Laine broke into a toothy grin and confidently agreed, his head still resting on the pillow. Sportsnet host

Daren Millard, who had been conducting the interview, seemed pleasantly shocked by Laine's candour: "I have to say, you're a cool cat here, really casual about this."

"Yeah, I know what I'm capable of and I know that I'm saying that," Laine replied in a Finnish drawl, "so I'm not afraid to say it out loud and like that about myself." Asked later about his sleepy performance, the Winnipeg Jets' second overall pick simply said, "It was filmed during the day. I was quite awake. I just wanted to be me in the interview and not have to pretend I was someone else."

Indeed, there is only one Laine. And he is definitely not boring or reserved. He speaks what's on his mind, often without a filter. On why he switched from being a goalie to a forward when he was twelve years old: "I'm afraid of pucks." On the success of his one-timer: "I will score ninety-nine times out of one hundred—the stick will break once." Although his lines are funny, they're also not very Finnish.

"First of all, I would check his passport," said former NHLer Ville Nieminen, who is from Laine's hometown of Tampere. "Check to see if he has a US passport, because he is cocky. He's not a typical Finnish guy. He's so self-confident. He's been following his own route."

In a cookie-cutter sport where hockey players are taught to spout clichés about "giving 110 per cent" and "taking it one day at a time," Laine arrived in the NHL like a breath of fresh air. Off the ice, he seemed more concerned with making reporters smile than necessarily saying the right thing. On the ice, he was Thor with a wicked one-timer—Finland's answer to Alex Ovechkin. "There isn't another player from here that has caused this kind of circus as Patrik," said Antti Makinen, a Finnish hockey broadcaster. "The driving school where Patrik got his licence, they are not marketing the driving school by their name. They are just putting his picture on a big poster. It says 'Our Patrik' and shows his licence. It's hilarious."

Laine's shtick wasn't always funny. Growing up in Finland, where the word "modesty" might as well be stitched into the country's coat of arms, Laine's swagger sometimes closed more doors than it opened. He was often benched for his bravado. He feuded with coaches and was kicked off the national team. He was accused of being a me-first player, the kind of teammate who would be smiling if he were scoring but would be cursing at himself and others if his shots weren't going in.

At the best of times, he was called immature. At the worst, he was accused of being selfish. The general feeling was that he wouldn't amount to much unless he conformed and became like every other player in the country. "There's been some times when I was younger where maybe the coach wants me to play like this, but I didn't feel like I kind of needed to, or I just wanted to play the way I wanted to play," said Laine. "If I tried to play my own way, I wasn't playing, or I was sitting on the bench or I was not even on the roster. There was

Patrik Laine started playing hockey at a young age. Photo courtesy of the Laine family

a season where I played like five games, because I wasn't ready to play the games that he wanted me to play, but I think that's only a good thing because there's millions of guys that can be that player that the coach wants them to be. But I didn't want to be that kind of player. I wanted to be my kind of player and develop that way."

Stubbornness served Laine well. Although he was often his own worst enemy—an emotional player who put the weight of the world on his shoulders to the point where he was assigned a full-time mental coach and needed to be talked out of quitting—he stuck to his guns to become one of his generation's deadliest snipers. In the process, he has become Finland's biggest and brashest star since Teemu Selänne was tossing his glove in the air and shooting it down with his stick. "I've been waiting a long time for Finland to bring another superstar to the league," said Selänne. "And finally we have one of them."

Of course, we have nothing to do with his shot. Nobody can teach a shot like that. As a coach you can say, "You should shoot a lot," or give him a couple of tips about shooting, but his shot is his own. Nobody has anything to do with his shot or his scoring.
— **JUSSI TAPOLA, head coach, Tappara Tampere**

THE NIGHTMARE-INDUCING shot, which netted him 36 goals as a rookie and 44 in 2017–18—second only to Alex Ovechkin in the Rocket Richard Trophy race—started innocently enough. In the backyard of his home, Laine had a hockey net, a bucket that held about fifty pucks and a board from which he would launch shot after shot. But most importantly, he had a neighbour who didn't appreciate it when hard, rubberized pucks would fly over the fence and hit his house. "I hardly missed," said Laine. "Just took shots in my backyard and learned how to shoot. I've always been a good shooter and always scored a lot of goals."

Shooting at a net soon got boring. So Laine's father would tie Coke cans to the top left and right corners of the crossbar. Together, they had a competition to see who could hit the most cans. But eventually, being able to hit the can wasn't enough. Accuracy, after all, is only one component of Laine's shot. So his dad replaced the cans with bottles and hung them from the top corners. For a player who ranked second in the hardest-shot competition at the

2017 NHL All-Star Game with a 101.7 mph blast, seeing the glass bottles explode and shower the ground with tiny bits of glass was almost as satisfying as scoring a goal.

At one time, Laine was also pretty good at preventing goals. From Miikka Kiprusoff to Tuukka Rask, Finland has a rich history of producing top-end goalies. Up until the age of twelve, a tall and lanky Laine dreamed of being the next Pekka Rinne until his father, who worked in Tampere as a plumber, decided Laine playing goalie was far too expensive and a waste of his son's natural talent. "I liked being goalie," said Laine. "Someone always had to go to the net. I just liked it, I don't know why. It was a long time ago. Nowadays, I would never be a goalie. Guys are shooting way too hard for me. It's nice to be a forward now."

No one taught Laine to shoot. No one even knows how he does it. Teammates have grabbed his stick, which has the elasticity of a pool noodle, and

Patrik Laine played in net until he was twelve, when he switched to playing forward. Photo courtesy of the Laine family

have wondered how he manages to generate so much power without snapping the thing in half. "I kind of figured it out on my own," said Laine. "I haven't practised techniques or stuff like that much. Just shooting and shooting. I don't know how I figured it out. It's pretty easy once you know how. I never had a skills coach helping me. I've been my own skills coach. I'm not teaching anyone. It's my secret."

For a while, Laine was Tampere's biggest secret. Located north of Helsinki in the southern part of Finland, Laine describes his hometown as "wet, cold and dark." Of course, it's like that in most of the country, especially in the winter. When Maple Leafs president Brendan Shanahan arrived in Finland for the 2016 World Junior Championship in December, he tweeted, "Early morning Helsinki... or mid-afternoon... or early evening" and then posted a picture of a sunless sky. Not surprisingly, Finns tend to consume more coffee—and alcohol—per capita than the residents of most other countries. They also consume a heck of a lot of hockey.

Tampere is at the centre of it all. Laine calls it "the home of Finnish hockey." It is here where the first hockey game was supposedly played, where the first indoor rink was built and where the country's Hockey Hall of Fame resides. Despite a population of less than 300,000, Tampere supports two professional hockey teams—Ilves and Tappara—and has graduated a number of players to the NHL, including Vesa Toskala, Jyrki Lumme and Aleksander Barkov. "I think everybody wants to be a hockey player in that town," said Laine, who grew up with three or four outdoor rinks within walking distance of his door.

Laine didn't work with the traditional skills coaches as a kid, but with a shot that could break Coke bottles, he quickly started getting attention as someone with a knack for the net. As a fourteen-year-old, he scored 28 goals and 45 points in 16 games for Tappara's U-16 team, as well as 17 goals and 26 points in 27 games for the U-18 B team. "I heard about him when he was a younger kid," said Jari Grönstrand, a Finnish-based scout for the Winnipeg Jets who is also from Tampere. "It was almost every game that he did something unbelievable. Some good goal or some good pass, and he can check too. He hits pretty hard. Maybe you haven't seen it yet in the NHL, but he can check. You didn't have to look for him on the ice."

Mostly, it was his shot that attracted the attention. He's always had it, even when he was playing goaltender and shooting pucks in the backyard. It came naturally, but he's put a lot of work into it, trying to make it harder, more accurate and—as he has said—more like Ovechkin's. "I've always been a good shooter and always scored a lot of goals. I don't know why," said Laine. "I watched a lot of videos on the Internet, trying to learn. I was always trying to improve my shot and improve my game."

"The passion is the number one thing," said Juha Juujärvi, Laine's coach in the Mestis league. "There are only a few young players in Finnish hockey that I have ever met or coached that have such big passion to score and such big passion to play with the puck. After every practice he wanted to play with the puck. Some players, when the practice ends, their eyes light up and they want to go. But Patrik was one of those guys who was still there every time wanting to play with the puck and shoot."

"I think the [biggest] strength that he has is he's such a worker," said Lauri Marjamäki, who was Finland's head coach at the World Cup of Hockey. "He's training with passion. He knows all the time what he needs. I'm sure he will be better next year than the previous year, because all the time he's thinking how he can improve his game and improve his body. There are a lot of good years coming with Patrik."

Laine stayed late after practice and spent hours in his backyard taking shots. But he also went to school. He studied Ovechkin's one-timer, breaking down YouTube clips so that he could get the puck to fly off his stick in the same manner. "It's timing and rhythm," Finnish-born skills coach Pertti Hasanen said of Laine's release. "He doesn't skate at all. It's just his arms and his core. You've got to flex your stick and then snap your shot off. He has that down to a science."

Laine wasn't just influenced by Ovechkin's shot. He loved everything about the Russian superstar—from his yellow tinted visor to the way he bounced off the boards to celebrate goals. Ovechkin was unlike any of the players Laine had grown up playing with or against. He was confident and cocky. Here was a player who would bang his stick on the ice to call for a pass, who would hang his leg over the bench tempting the coach to put him into the game, who took as many shots as he wanted. Ovechkin wasn't just the best player, he also knew he was the best player.

It wasn't that the Washington Capitals sniper was selfish. He just knew that if the team needed a goal, he was the one who should have the puck on his stick. Laine started to think the same way. He wanted to be the go-to guy. He loved the feeling of scoring, but even more than that he loved the feeling of being counted on to help his team win games. And like Ovechkin, he wasn't shy about pounding his chest.

It wasn't just his goal-scoring exploits that attracted scouts. He was tall and lanky and liked to use his impressive size to dole out hits—something that other kids just weren't doing. Plus, he really liked to celebrate his success, often jumping against the glass and pumping his fist after a goal. In a country where the mood of the people resembled the weather—overcast and lacking in sunshine—this stood out almost as much as his powerful shot.

"If I want to do something, I'm going to do it," said Laine. "I'm not going to ask everybody else. But obviously in a good way. I'm not going to do anything stupid just because I want to do it." There's stubbornness there. There's also a confidence. Both got Laine into trouble at times.

In Europe, where the ice surface is much larger and the game resembles a soccer match, a shoot-first mentality is a foreign concept. Players are taught to work the puck around, like pieces on a chessboard, waiting for an opening to attack. Laine took a more aggressive approach, even if it didn't always lead to victory. "From the age of probably fourteen he was trying to shoot from every angle and trying the one-timer," said Jonatan Tanus, a former teammate. "Right now, he's maybe thinking a little more when to shoot. But back then, he was shooting from pretty much everywhere."

"There was a little bit of noise about how he was so individual," said Grönstrand. "I don't know much about what happened then, but when you're a young kid you make some mistakes. When he went to the big team and started to play there, he changed a lot. He started to grow up."

To North Americans, Laine is another Teemu Selänne. But in Finland, where his face is already on billboards, he is much more. He represents a new generation and a new wave of thinking. It's okay to celebrate and have fun. Teamwork is still important, but in today's NHL, you cannot win without individual game-breakers. Laine didn't always back up his words. Earlier on, he sometimes made noise for the wrong reasons. A defining moment in his career occurred at the 2014 Ivan Hlinka Memorial Tournament, when he was kicked off his team for reportedly threatening to kill his coach for not playing him. According to Laine, it didn't exactly happen that way.

Finland, which finished fifth in the tournament, had been playing the US for a chance to go to the semifinal. But Laine, who had been prone to giveaways and high-risk plays, couldn't get off the bench and his team lost 9–4. He finished with 1 goal in 3 games. He was frustrated and lost it. After the end of the game, Laine removed his glove and gave the middle finger to the coach when he wasn't looking. But Laine said he didn't threaten his life, just told a couple of teammates that he'd sure like to punch him or something, which got the broken telephone treatment when reporters caught wind of what happened. "It was big news, actually," said Finnish reporter Juha Hiitelä. "I think it started as pretty small news, but then when people started to realize what was said and that it was something that doesn't normally happen, it became a bigger story."

"Yeah, that was kind of a tough spot for a teenager to handle," said Laine. "But if you think about it now, I think it's only a good thing that it happened, because at the time I noticed the not-so-fun side of media. It wasn't funny at all. I've seen that when I was young. It made me careful."

I think mentally he was wanting to win every game. And he was mad at himself if he didn't score goals and when he was mad at himself he then started yelling at parents and coaches and everyone else. But it was because he wanted to win. That's all he wanted.

— **MARKO OJANEN, assistant coach, Tappara Tampere**

HOW DID LAINE GO FROM GETting kicked off national and club teams to winning the World Junior Championship and being named MVP in the top Finnish league? He grew up. And he got help. But before that, he had to take another step backward. At sixteen years old, Laine was not good enough to play for Tappara's main team in the SM-liiga (the Finnish elite league) but he was also too good to go back to junior. So Tappara loaned him to LeKi in the second division, where he could still play against men and develop. It was supposed to be an easy transition, but it ended up becoming one of the most difficult—and important—years in Laine's career.

From the very beginning, his reputation as a problem child preceded him. "I didn't know him," said Juha Juujärvi, a coach with LeKi. "I talked to the coach with Tappara's main team and they said they had a young, talented guy and to take care of him. There was huge media because Patrik had some problems with the national team. Tappara said that they wanted to help him."

Laine struggled at the start. The moves that had worked against junior-aged players no longer worked when playing against men. He was trying too much on his own, taking too many shots and causing too many turnovers. He was also putting too much pressure on himself. In his mind, he was there to develop, which meant he was there to score goals and win games. When he didn't do that, he tried to force matters and ended up playing even worse. Laine scored 5 goals and 7 assists in 36 games that season, but he was also a minus-12.

To help Laine understand just how much he was hurting the team with his selfish play, Juujärvi began printing off game reports and highlighting two columns: shots and turnovers. "Patrik led in shots almost every time. He would shoot about eight times every game," said Juujärvi. "But turnovers were bad for him—even ten sometimes. He had so many turnovers and it caused so many problems, like what the fuck's he doing? Why didn't he pass or put the puck in deep? He always wanted to win one-on-one situations."

For Laine, it was a dark time. He knew he was letting the team down. But he also knew he was letting himself down. The goals weren't coming as easily as they had previously. After the Ivan Hlinka tournament, he was getting a reputation as a player you couldn't win with. The more he struggled, the more he tried to do everything on his own. It kept snowballing until he felt like the weight of the world was on his shoulders.

Juujärvi took a tough approach. He cared about Laine and wanted to see him tap the potential that everyone could see he had, but Juujärvi also knew that unless Laine was willing to put the team ahead of his own points, the youngster would never achieve his goal of making the NHL. After a 3–2 loss in which Laine had turned the puck over in the second period for the winning goal, Juujärvi sat Laine on the bench and told him, "You will not play anymore today. I don't want to see that kind of hockey ever."

It was like a father telling his son that he had disappointed him. Laine didn't say anything back. He knew he had cost the team the win, knew that he was failing, knew that his chances of making the NHL were quickly slipping through his fingers. On the bus ride back to Tampere, a sixteen-year-old Laine was so upset that he told another player that he wanted to quit. Nothing was working. The more he tried, the worse it got.

Before it got better, it got even worse. LeKi had qualified as the last seed for the playoffs. But with the series tied 1–1, Juujärvi made Laine a healthy scratch for Game 3, not trusting that Laine could play a mistake-free game. The team won and Laine returned to Tappara's junior team. Fourteen months later, he would lead Tappara's main team to a league championship, winning playoff MVP. But at the time, some wondered where his career was heading. "To be honest, everyone saw the potential," said Tanus, "but I would think it would probably take three years more."

"We never destroyed his dream," said Juujärvi. "We cared about him. I saw every time that he wanted to develop and he got better and better." Indeed, Laine didn't quit. And Tappara didn't give up on him. Instead, they challenged him to get fitter and faster. He cut out ice cream (though he would have half a bowl of Skittles ice cream to celebrate his first NHL hat trick) and worked with a power skating coach to refine a labouring stride.

"His skating was a big issue. He's a big guy and he grew fast," said Tappara head coach Jussi Tapola. "His skating was very lousy. He couldn't skate in the league. What we did was work with him on the technical skills with how he turns and how fast he can be with the first step."

In addition to his speed, the team also worked on his psyche. It seemed to be even more flawed. Laine started working with a mental coach. Even more than his deadly shot, it might be the reason why he's in the NHL today. "That's the thing exactly. I'm actually very hard on myself," said Laine. "I'm assuming that every time I'm on the ice that I need to score. Every shot I take I need to score. It's hard sometimes but I think it's only a good thing that you are hard on yourself because you're pushing yourself." Those expectations were amplified at the lower levels, where Laine knew he was being counted on to produce offensively. At times, it became a burden.

Laine spent a full year with the mental coach by his side. They talked before and after games. The main topic of conversation was Laine's offensive production and the mountains of pressure he put on himself to score. Up until then, Laine believed he was put on the ice for just one purpose: to put the puck in the net. If he scored, he believed he had played a good game regardless of whether the team won or lost. If he didn't score, he felt like a failure. "It was the worst game for me," was a common Laine phrase, even after a win.

The mental coach explained he was looking at it wrong. Scoring was obviously important, but it represented a snapshot of the entire picture. It was what you did when you were not scoring that truly defined you as a player. "He told me that when you score, it's only a couple of seconds out of your ice time during the game," said Laine. "So if you play nineteen minutes, you have to play 18:55 the proper way. You have to do all the little things on the ice when you're not scoring. You can help your team to win when you're not scoring. You can do a lot of good things still. That's the thing I tried to remember the past couple of years, that I can help my team to win even if I'm not scoring."

Tapola also helped with the mental side. He stripped away any and all expectations from Laine. What Tapola wanted—what he expected—was for Laine to understand the rhythm of the game. There is a time to try going around a player in a one-on-one situation and there is a time to shoot, but there are also times where the best play is to dump the puck in deep and cut your losses. "We always knew that if he got the mental side of the game and he understood how to play the game, he would be a top player in the SM-liiga and in the NHL," said Tapola. "But it always was the mental side of the game. He was frustrated all the time and it was up and down all game."

Tapola also introduced Laine to a technique called "shot-blocking" which previously had been a foreign concept to a forward who rarely ventured into the defensive zone. The adjustments weren't easy. Laine had been a high-stakes gambler his entire life and now he was told to play the penny slots? It took some learning. "We lost some games because of him," said Tapola. "It was like his junior games. But when we talked about that, we told him he has everything—he has the skills—but he had to understand the momentums of the game. He understood that he wants to play a big part in the game and play in the last minute and be the guy scoring goals."

Tapola wasn't just teaching "boring" defence. Tapola's greatest strength as a coach was recognizing what he had in Laine. His shot was special. You don't limit that—you exploit it. Whereas other coaches had benched him for what they viewed as "giving up the puck," Tapola encouraged him to fire at will as long as there was traffic in front of the net.

That often wasn't a problem. "He's the kind of guy who when he gets over the blue line, he mostly shoots," said Tapola. "If there's a guy who's going to the net, it's good that he shoots. But if there's no one that's going to the net, then he should do something else. Of course, the guys that played with him would accelerate to the net as soon as they crossed the blue line. Nobody has a shot like that. Even if the goaltender stops it, he gives him good rebounds and stuff like that. The goalies can't handle it. When you have a player like that, you have to play differently. And it's smart to play differently."

Laine scored 17 goals and 33 points in 46 games for Tappara, but it was after returning as a hero from the World Junior Championship that his season really took off. "He was an absolute monster," teammate Nick Plastino said of Laine's playoff run, in which he scored 10 goals and 15 points in 18 games to lead the team to a championship. "I remember some guys telling me in training camp that there was this young kid named Patrik Laine and that he was a good player, but wasn't the best skater and how he couldn't make the team the previous year," said Plastino. "I didn't really notice him at first. But as the year went on, I don't know what he did but he was unbelievable. He peaked so fast. I guess he finally figured out that he was that good and that he could take that next step."

It wasn't that Laine realized he was that good. It was that the team finally did. By the end of the year, Laine had not only become the best player in the country, he was setting himself up to be the second overall pick in the draft. "He's not always listening to the coach," said Tanus. "He was never asking questions to the coach. He knows he's good and he was doing what he thinks is the best. And that's how he proved himself. He showed everyone that he is a great player and a superstar."

"The focus used to be on systems and team play. Now, the focus is on individual skill and how you read and react. You just have to play the game like it's supposed to be played. You have to make decisions by yourself and read and react and do things accordingly. The focus is on individuals more than on team play. Patrik Laine was part of that."

— **JUKKA JALONEN, Finland's 2015 World Junior Championship coach**

OF COURSE, TEEMU SELÄNNE WAS WAITING FOR LAINE. HE had just seen Finland win gold at the World Junior Championship and, standing in the bowels of Hartwall Arena, where a couple of days earlier he had been inducted into the International Ice Hockey Federation Hall of Fame, Selänne was waiting to shake the hand of the player he called "the future of Finnish hockey."

When the World Junior Championship had begun a few weeks earlier, no one could have expected that Finland would win gold or that a pair of seventeen-year-olds—Laine and Jesse

Puljujärvi—who were too young to order a pint of Lapin Kulta premium lager and still had to wear full face masks, would be leading the tournament in scoring. As most observers had said, it was too bad Finland had to be hosting this year when the team was so young and so raw.

Expectations were low for Laine and Puljujärvi as they were heading into a tournament that was typically dominated by nineteen-year-olds. "We wanted them to play with confidence and not worry about making mistakes," said coach Jukka Jalonen. "Just enjoy the game and have fun. They really did that." Jalonen put Laine and Puljujärvi together because "they were both in their draft year, so they wanted to help each other succeed." But they needed a centre. That's where Sebastian Aho, who would later join the NHL with the Carolina Hurricanes, fit in. A natural winger, he moved to the middle where his primary goal was to get Laine the puck.

"I think they're brothers somehow," teammate Kasperi Kapanen said of Laine, Puljujärvi and Aho. "They're just not telling us that they're brothers. They just know where each other are and I just laugh on the bench when they score. I've never seen anything like it before."

That Laine was good enough to dominate against players who were as much as two years older was just one part of the equation. The other part was Jalonen. Canada had been conservative with its underage players in the tournament. Finland did the opposite. Realizing that the team's youngsters were its best players, the coaching staff loosened the reins on them and just let them play. For Laine, it was the first time he was allowed to be himself. "If you over-coach them, you will make a mistake," said Jalonen. "Obviously they will make some mistakes, but if you try to correct them all the time and they start thinking all over the ice, it's bad. So you have to let them play."

It made for some wild hockey. In a back-and-forth game against Canada, Laine scored the game-winner on a slapshot that seemed to go through goaltender Mackenzie Blackwood. Laine finished the tournament ranked third in scoring with 7 goals and 13 points in 7 games—behind Puljujärvi (17 points) and Aho (14 points). "It was one of those rare experiences," said Jalonen. "Once in a while, you have a line on the club team where you can sit back. You can't teach the skills of those offensive players. Talent doesn't automatically mean that three guys can click together and play together. It doesn't always happen. But with those guys, it really worked so well."

The win was a huge turning point in Laine's career. Laine had always been full of swagger. But now it was justified. He was being encouraged to use the shot that so many had previously tried to tame. He won a league title and was named to Finland's world championship team, where he was the MVP of the tournament, and then played at the World Cup before he even made his NHL debut. That he did it his own way made the ascent even sweeter.

"He rose up like a rocket, more or less," said Goran Stubb, the European-based scout for NHL Central Scouting. "Two, three years ago he wasn't outstanding. But when you get to know him a little bit, you realize that his will and his ambitions are not normal. He wants so much and he's willing to work hard for these goals. He was practising his shot all year round. It was a great year for him."

When you get an opportunity to draft in the top end of the draft, those are the type of players that can make a difference. Every year is different, so you don't know exactly what that player is going to do moving forward. But from what I've seen at the top end of the draft, these are players that can make an impact over a period of time. No one player is going to change a franchise overnight. But certainly it is a big building piece and building block moving forward.

— **KEVIN CHEVELDAYOFF, Winnipeg Jets general manager, April 2016**

KEVIN CHEVELDAYOFF WAS IN FINLAND FOR THE WORLD Junior Championship, but perhaps wisely didn't stay for the after-party that shut down the country. "I've heard stories from guys that stayed," said the Winnipeg Jets GM, laughing. "I wouldn't want anyone doing any work on my brakes, or anything like that on my car the next day, that's for sure." At the time of the tournament, Cheveldayoff wasn't in Helsinki on a scouting mission. He couldn't have imagined that the Jets would finish low enough to select Laine or Puljujärvi or even a player in the top ten. He was simply there to watch his team's prospects. Even so, he couldn't keep his eyes off what the two kids from Finland were doing.

"You knew that whoever was going to get an opportunity to draft any of those players was going to be fortunate." When the Jets missed the playoffs and then won the second overall pick in the draft lottery—jumping up four spaces—one of the first calls Cheveldayoff made was to Finland-based scout Jari Grönstrand. "What do you think?" Cheveldayoff asked.

"I said that he can be a forty-, fifty-, sixty-goal scorer. He's that good," said Grönstrand. As for the other factors—the criticisms that Laine was immature and selfish—Grönstrand was not worried in the least. He was from Laine's hometown. He knew Laine's parents. His wife was a teacher where Laine went to school. "It was blown out of proportion," he said. The kid would give the team zero problems.

"From a personal standpoint, we certainly did do a lot of due diligence," said Cheveldayoff. "The more we spent time with Patrik and talked with people about Patrik, the more excited we got as an organization. You really began to understand what drives him, what he is, who he is. It's like, 'Okay, now I get that interview [that he did at the draft lottery with Sportsnet].' There's just a 'I am who I am, and I'm just going to go play hockey' type of mentality. He's not in this for you. He's in this to be the player that he believes he can be and that's all. At the end of the day, Patrik is a very, very driven person who wants to be the best."

CONCLUSION

THEIR STORIES ARE DIFFERENT. BUT THEY ARE PRETTY much all the same. If you haven't already realized it by now, go back and read them again. Whether it was McDavid weaving through paint cans or Matthews showing up to the rink with a duffle bag full of different-coloured jerseys or Eichel hanging pictures of his role models—and rivals—on his bedroom door, the same underlying theme runs throughout each origin story.

You need to be driven to succeed. You need talent, sure. But it's not nearly enough. The players in this book are not just good NHLers; they are some of the best rising stars, something they achieved through practice, passion and perseverance—almost to the point of obsession.

What's the big difference between McDavid and his older brother? Connor felt like he had to take one hundred shots every day. Why did Johnny Gaudreau make it to the NHL, whereas his father ended up a really good college player? Johnny didn't listen to the doubters who said he was too small. There have been first-overall flops and can't-miss prospects who have missed their mark. But while analysts were questioning Scheifele's future or wondering if Laine had the mental maturity to realize his potential, the players themselves were putting in the work to get to where they wanted to be.

It wasn't a fluke. No one actually wakes up one day with superhero abilities. Even for the so-called "phenoms," it takes time and effort and all the things that most of us are not prepared to invest.

There are sacrifices made, obstacles to overcome and critics to answer to. It's a lesson for the next generation of young stars, many of whom are already writing their origin stories. We can't wait to read them.

ACKNOWLEDGEMENTS

NONE OF THE PLAYERS IN THIS BOOK WOULD BE IN the NHL without the support of their families and the same applies to me. Thank you Mom, Dad and Chris for being my biggest fans. Thank you Danielle for your love and support (even if you are quite slow at transcribing) and thank you Madison and Joshua for being really quiet when Daddy was conducting interviews on the phone. I would also like to thank the players in the book for allowing me to properly tell their stories, as well as their parents, friends, agents, coaches, teammates for being open and honest. A special thank-you goes out to my former sports editors Jim Bray and Bev Wake, for taking a chance on me so long ago. And to my current Sports Editor, Bill Pierce, a big thanks for your daily email emojis, which always put a much-needed smile on my face, and for thinking I'm a "normal guy." Last, but certainly not least, thank you to my agent, Brian Wood, for pushing me to write something—anything—as well as the kind people at Harbour Publishing Co. Ltd./Douglas and McIntyre for making this possible, and in particular to Brianna Cerkiewicz, for being really, really patient with me during this entire process.

CREDITS

Eichel quote on page 126: Courtesy of *Sports Illustrated*.

Marner quote on page 169: Material republished with the express permission of: *Toronto Sun*, a division of Postmedia Network Inc.

Marner quote on page 170: Material republished with the express permission of: *National Post*, a division of Postmedia Network Inc.

Karlsson quote on page 174: Material republished with the express permission of: *Ottawa Citizen*, a division of Postmedia Network Inc.

Millard Sportsnet interview on pages 197–198: Used with permission of Rogers Media Inc. All rights reserved.

Cheveldayoff quote on page 213: Courtesy of NHL.com.

INDEX

Numbers in **bold** indicate an image

Sun County Panthers, 70, 72,
79, 80, 81

Tallon, Dale, 87–88
Tanus, Jonatan, 204–5,
208, 211
Tapola, Jussi, 200, 208,
209–210
Tavares, John, 69, 82, 188
Team Canada, 1, 5
Team North America, 1, 189,
191, 192
Ted Lindsay Award, 2, 130
Timashov, Dmytro, 101
Tkachuk, Matthew, 169,
184, 185
Toronto Maple Leafs, 5, 24, 57,
90, 94, 104, 136, 150–
54, 157, 160, 168–74,
189, 190, 193, 202
Torrie, Dave, 49, 61–62

United States Hockey League
(USHL), 26, 35, 37.
*See also specific
teams*

Vegas Golden Knights, 7

Weiss, Bob, 96–97
Western Conference, 36–37
Wilkes-Barre/Scranton
Penguins. *See
Scranton Penguins*
Winnipeg Jets, 4, 6, 7, 20, 21,
22, 175, 196, 198, 202,
213, 214
World Cup of Hockey, 1, 189,
191, 192, 203
world juniors, 41–42, 59,
78, 166
2013, 43
2015, 147, 185
2016, 101, 185, 202, 210,
211, 214

York, Jerry, 40, 41, 42, 43

About the
AUTHOR

MICHAEL TRAIKOS has been writing about hockey for two decades. He is the National Hockey Writer for Postmedia News and his daily columns and feature stories are published in every major city across the country. He covered the Toronto Maple Leafs as the beat reporter for the *National Post*, and he is a regular contributor to *The Hockey News*. He lives in Newmarket, ON, on a street not far from where Connor McDavid used to shoot pucks on his driveway.